TO TRAIN UP A CHILD

Child Training for the 21st Century

Michael and Debi Pearl

To Train Up a Child: Child Training for the 21st Century

Publication date: May 2015

Print: ISBN: 978-1-61644-072-5
eBook: ISBN: 978-1-61644-073-2
ePub: ISBN: 978-1-61644-074-9

All Scripture quotations are taken from the King James Holy Bible

Library of Congress Control Number: 2015937790

This publication is designed to provide accurate and authoritative information in regard to the subject matter covered. It is sold with the understanding that the author or the publisher is not engaged in rendering any type of professional services. If expert assistance is required, the services of a competent professional should be sought.

1. Child Training 2. Children 3. Parenting 4. Homeschooling 5. Obedience 6. Religion 7. Jesus 8. Christianity
I. Pearl, Michael; Pearl, Debi II. To Train Up a Child: Child Training for the 21st Century Revised & Expanded

To Train Up a Child: Child Training for the 21st Century may be purchased at special quantity discounts for churches, donor programs, fund raising, book clubs, or educational purposes for churches, congregations, schools and universities. Rights and Licensing in other languages and international sales opportunities are available. For more information contact:

Mel Cohen
1000 Pearl Road
Pleasantville TN 37033
(931) 593-2484
mcohen@nogreaterjoy.org

Cover and interior design by Aaron Aprile
Cover Photograph by Lynne Hopwood
Printed in the United States of America

Publisher: No Greater Joy Ministries, Inc.
www.nogreaterjoy.org

Foreword

To Train Up a Child, first published in 1994, began as a letter to a homeschool mother in answer to her question, "How did you train your children to be so happy and obedient?" I did not consider myself to be an author, nor did I possess the means or the knowledge to publish a book. But as I sat down to write a letter to this mother, I realized that it was a big subject that could not be put into a few pages. I consulted my friends and neighbors, gleaning their views and methods of child training. I even interviewed my children, asking them what they thought about their upbringing. Deb and I analyzed how we were influenced by the traditions we inherited from our parents, and we looked at the methods that were unique to our family. Friends and members of our church periodically read and critiqued the manuscript as it grew to book size.

After about two years, that mother finally got a response. So I want to thank Penny Mullen for asking the right question. Twenty years later, *To Train Up a Child* has sold over 1.2 million copies in twelve languages. TTUAC has been on Amazon's best-seller list several times.

For the past 19 years we have published a bimonthly magazine, *No Greater Joy,* and written a number of books speaking to the needs of the family. We have received tens of thousands of letters of gratitude and been approached by thousands of young people thanking us for our influence in the way they were raised—their parents having implemented the principles expressed in TTUAC. We are humbled to have played a part.

Our children are all grown, ranging from 31 to 41 years of age. They have given us 22 grandchildren so far, with two more on the way. They love God and are great parents, fully supportive of their parents, employing us as babysitters on a regular basis. Our home remains full of little running feet and is regularly strewn with books and toys. I am teaching a new generation of boys and girls how to fish and throw knives. Deb is teaching the girls how to cook and garden. I am now Big Papa and Deb is Mama Pearl.

Our magazine always contains articles written by our children. They often have insights that surpass their parents'. Rebekah and Shoshanna are published authors. Shoshanna is a speaker at herb conventions. Shalom is a popular speaker at homeschool conventions and ladies' meetings. Nathan is a Bible teacher and public speaker. He is presently teaching the Bible in a small college. Gabriel is a businessman, a great father who worships God, and is an active participant in church activities.

When I read back over this book, I was shocked at some of the poor writing of 21 years ago. So I edited the entire book. The content is identical, with some additions. Those of you who are already familiar with the original book will not notice the differences, except for one new chapter. I changed a few adverbs and adjectives, rearranged some sentences to make them active instead of passive, and updated terminology to accommodate the evolving connotation of popular words and phrases. I have also added clarifying phrases or sentences in some instances. The most appreciable difference is a large section on the modern move to make corporal chastisement illegal. And I have done significant editing and made some additions to the subject of guilt and self-loathing.

There has been no editing to modify our stance on spanking. To the contrary, due to the media attacks, I have expanded and strengthened our arguments for traditional, biblical child training. I intend to be the last man standing. If I am in my grave, there are more than a million books circulating in the United States that will continue to stand for traditional, biblical parenting.

Table of Contents

Train up a child in the way
he should go: and when he is old,
he will not depart from it.

Proverbs 22:6

CHAPTER 1

To Train Up a Child

SWITCH YOUR KIDS

When you tell some parents they need to switch their children, they respond, "I would if I could find someone willing to trade." I have had children in my house who were enough to give an electric wheat grinder a nervous breakdown. Their parents looked like escapees from a WWII Polish boxcar. Another hour with those kids and I would have been searching the yellow pages for discount vasectomies. While we tried to sit and talk, the children were constantly running in and out of doors, complaining of ill treatment from the others, begging to go or stay or eat, or demanding a toy that another child would not relinquish. The mother had to continually jump up and rescue some breakable object. She said, "No," 666 times in the space of two hours. She swatted each child two or three times—usually with her hand on top of a diaper. Other than misaligning the child's spine, it seemed to have no effect—understandably so.

When we suggest to permissive parents that they should respond to certain transgressions with physical chastisement (not a karate chop to the lower backbone), some mothers can only visualize themselves further brutalizing their children, thinking it will do no good anyway! Their "discipline" is just "laying down a field of fire" to give themselves sufficient cover to get through to the next task. They have no hope of conquering the child's stubborn will. They just desire to create enough diversion to accomplish their own mission. It is a fact that spankings administered by frustrated parents are as counterproductive as not spanking when it is needful.

Another mother walked into my house with her little ones and sat down to talk. She said to them, "Go out in the sunroom and play, and don't bother Mama unless you need something." For the next two hours we were not even aware the children were present, except when a little one came in holding herself saying, "Pee-pee, Mama." They played together well, resolved their own conflicts, and didn't expect indulgent pacification when one of the girls turned the rocking horse over, bumping her head. They didn't run in and out, tearing the place apart—*they were told not to.*

This mother did not spank her children while at my house, nor did she need to rebuke them. She looked rested. When she called the children to go home, one little fellow asked, "Mama, can I stay and play with Shoshanna?" Mother answered, "No, not today. We have work to do at home." As he lifted his arms, his mother picked him up. Hugging his mother's neck, he said, "I love you, Mama."

This young mother said to me, "My children want to please me. They try so hard to do everything I say. We have such fun together." She is looking forward to having more children. They are the joy of her life.

By the grace of God and through the simple and practical biblical principles found in these pages, and with determination and an open heart, this mother has trained up children who bring her joy and honor. You can do the same.

OBEDIENCE TRAINING

Most parenting is reactive, the opposite of proactive. Children are left to their own devices until their actions are irritating, and then parents verbally or physically whip them back into line. A clear-thinking parent will feel uncomfortable with this approach but may not know that there is an alternative that is more comfortable and effective for both the parent and the child. We are talking about proactive training.

Many parents don't think little children can be trained, but training doesn't necessarily require that the trainee be capable of reason. Even mice and rats can be trained to respond to stimuli. Careful training can make a dog perfectly obedient. And all the dog training books tell us that a well-trained dog is a lot more content than one allowed to do as he pleases. The same is true of a child.

You think your kids are too little, do you? If a seeing-eye dog can be trained to reliably lead a blind man through the dangers of city streets, shouldn't a parent expect more out of an intelligent one-year-old? A dog can be trained not to touch a tasty morsel laid in front of him. Can't a child be trained not to touch? A dog can be trained to come, stay, sit, be quiet, or fetch upon command. You may not have trained your dog that well, yet every day someone accomplishes it on the dumbest of mutts. You think you are not qualified to be a trainer? Even a clumsy teenager can be trained to be an effective trainer in a dog obedience school.

Training must be proactive. If you wait until your dog is displaying unacceptable behavior before you rebuke (or kick) him, you will have a foot-shy mutt that is always skulking around to see what he can get away with before being screamed at. Where there is an absence of training, you can no more rebuke and whip a child into acceptable behavior than you can the family dog. No amount of discipline—and that includes spanking—can make up for a lack of training.

Proper training always works with every child. To neglect training is to create miserable circumstances for you and your children. Out of ignorance, many have bypassed training and expected discipline alone to effect proper behavior. It hasn't worked, and it never will.

"TENNN—HUTT!!"

When headstrong young men join the military, the first thing they are taught is to stand still. The many hours of close-order drill are designed to teach and reinforce *submission of the will*. "Attention!" pronounced, "TENNN—HUTT!!" is the beginning of all military maneuvers. A sergeant can call his men to attention and then ignore them, and without further explanation or command they will continue to stand frozen in that position until they fall out unconscious. The maneuvers "Right flank, left flank, companeeey—halt!" have no value in war except that they condition the men to instant, unquestioning obedience. Their will is not broken but their willfulness is. Just think of the relief that it would bring if by one command you could gain the absolute, focused attention of all your children.

As in the military, all maneuvers in the home should begin with a call to attention. Three-fourths of all home discipline problems would be solved if you could instantly gain your children's silent, unmoving attention. "TO THE REAR—MARCH" translated into family language would be: "Leave the room," or "Go to bed." Without question they would turn and go. This is normal in the well-trained family. And that degree of order and obedience brings peace and security to the children thus trained. I am not suggesting a militarized atmosphere, just a comparable level of respectful compliance.

"WHOA, HORSE"

Though we drive vehicles, we live in a horse-and-buggy community where someone is always training a new horse. When you get into a buggy to go down a narrow, winding state highway filled with eighteen-wheelers and logging trucks, you must have a totally submissive horse. You cannot depend on whipping him into submission after he willfully does what he shouldn't. One mistake and the young men will again be making several new pine boxes and digging six-foot-deep holes in the orchard.

The first thing you train a horse to do is to stand still and submit to being caught and handled. He must not fear the bridle or harness. He must stand still while thirteen children step in front of the iron wheels to climb into the buggy. When stopped at the end of a driveway waiting for the traffic to clear, he must not exercise his will to step out in front of eighty thousand pounds of speeding truck.

Horse training involves preparing the horse to respond correctly in all future situations to which he will be exposed. This proactive training takes place in a controlled environment where circumstances are purposefully created to test and condition the horse's responses. This is done by taking him through various paces. To train him to stop, you hold the bridle as you lead the horse and say, "Whoa," and then stop. Since you have a tight hold on the bridle, he must stop. After just a few times, the horse will stop at only the command. **The goal of all training is to quickly move beyond the use of force and constraint. Horses are not trained until they willingly respond.** Again, their will is not broken, rather; it is directed to voluntarily submit to authority, a condition that brings peace to both a horse and a child.

The trainer establishes the tone of voice that provokes a response from the horse. If you speak in a normal tone, the horse will learn to obey at that level. If you scream "Whoa!!" when training him, then in the future he will not stop unless you scream the same way. One farmer I know trained his horses with a wild, frantic bellow. Most of his neighbors who speak quietly to their animals find it difficult to control his horses because of their inability to raise their voices in such vehemence.

SPEAK TO ME ONLY

I was logging once with a fifteen-hundred-pound mule that sometimes wanted to run away with the log. In moments of stress (I was actually panic-stricken), I found myself frantically YELLING commands. The owner would patiently caution me, "Speak quietly and calmly or he will pay no attention." I never did learn the art of calmly saying "Whoa" to a runaway mule pulling a twenty-five-foot white oak log downhill with my foot hung in the trace chain. The point to remember is that animals learn to identify not only the sound but also the tone.

If you raise your voice when giving a command to your child, he will learn to associate your tone and volume with your intention. If you have trained him to respond to a bellow, don't blame him if he ignores your first thirteen calm "suggestions" while waiting for your fevered pitch to reach the point where he interprets it to be a real command with expectations attached.

TRAINING, NOT DISCIPLINE

"Train up a child in the way he should go: and when he is old, he will not depart from it" (Prov. 22:6). Train up—not beat up. Train up—not discipline up. Train up—not educate up. Train up—not "positive affirmation" up. **Training is the element most often missed in child rearing.** A child needs more than obedience training, but **without first training him, discipline is insufficient.**

Parents should not wait until their child's behavior becomes unacceptable before commencing training—which would then actually be discipline (in the modern connotation). **Training is not discipline.** Discipline is the "damage control" part of training, but it is insufficient in itself to effect proper behavior. Training is the conditioning of the child's mind *before* the crisis arises. It is preparation for future, instant, unquestioning obedience. An athlete trains before he competes. Animals, including wild ones, are conditioned to respond to the trainer's voice, or even hand signals.

The frustration parents experience is a result of their failure to train. Their problem is not "bad" children, just bad training. The strong-willed, the hyperactive, the highly intelligent, the special needs, and the easily bored all need training, and training is effective on all.

Understand, at this point we are not talking about producing godly children, just happy and obedient children. The principles for training young children to instantly obey can be applied by non-Christians as well as Christians. Although, as children get older, when *more is caught than taught,* the character, example, and admonition of the trainer play a more significant role.

TRAINING NOT TO TOUCH

There is a lot of satisfaction to be gained in training up a child. It is easy, yet challenging. When my children were able to crawl (in the case of one, roll) around the room, I set up training sessions. Just as one trains a horse by fabricating situations that simulate real-life challenges, parents can best train a child by setting aside time to be fully focused on training. Furthermore, there are some things we must teach children outside of real-life experiences because of the danger of their making the wrong choice later—like touching a hot stove, or picking up broken glass.

Try it yourself. Place an appealing object where they can reach it, maybe in a "no-no" corner or on the carrot juice table (another name for the coffee table). When they spy it and make a dive for it, in a calm voice say, "No, don't touch that." Since they are already familiar with the word "No," they will likely pause, look at you in wonder, and then turn around and grab it. Switch their hand once and simultaneously say, "No." Remember, in this exercise you are not disciplining, you are training. One spat with a little switch (pencil, wooden spoon, rubber spatula, etc.) is enough. It should not be hard enough to make them cry. When children become emotional, the cognitive part of the brain shuts down and you cannot train them until they are relaxed again. The little spat will cause them to again pull back their hand and consider the relationship between the object—their desire—the command, and the little reinforcing pain. It may take several times, but if you are consistent, they will learn to consistently obey commands even in your absence.

PLANT YOUR TREE IN THE MIDST OF THE GARDEN

When God wanted to train his first two children to obey, He placed a forbidden object within their reach. The forbidden tree was not inherently dangerous. It had no meaning until God used it as a prop to teach obedience. So He placed the *"tree of the knowledge of good and evil"* in the *"midst of the garden"* (Gen. 3:3) where they would be exposed to its temptation more often. God's purpose was not to save the tree, but to train the couple to exercise their wills in the art of self-denial and obedience.

Note that the name of the tree was not just "knowledge of evil," but, "knowledge of **good** and **evil**." By exercising their wills not to eat, they would have learned the meaning of *good* as well as *evil*. Eating the tree's fruit was not the only way in which they could have come to knowledge of good and evil. It was a fabricated shortcut that would most favorably facilitate the exercise of their wills and test their obedience.

By placing a forbidden object within reach of the children, and then enforcing your command to not touch it, every time the children pass the no-no object (their "tree of the knowledge of good and evil"), they are gaining knowledge of *good* and *evil* from the standpoint of an overcomer. As with Adam and Eve in the garden, the touching of the object, in itself, is of no consequence; but the attachment of a command to it makes it a moral "factory" where character is developed. By your enforcement, your children are learning about moral government, duty, responsibility, and, in the event of failure, accountability, rewards, and punishment. In the here and now they are also learning not to touch, which makes a child a much more pleasant member of the social group.

It just takes a few minutes to train a child not to touch a given object. Most children can be brought into complete and joyous compliance in just a few minutes. Thereafter, if you are consistent, the children will remain happy and obedient. By obedient, I mean, you will hardly ever need to tell them twice, and you will seldom find it necessary to resort to swatting or spanking. If you expect to receive instant obedience, and you train them to that end, you will be successful. It will take extra time to train, but once the children are in general subjection, the time saved will be extraordinary. Some people say, "Child-proof your home." I say, "Home-proof your child."

TOUCHY SITUATIONS

Have you ever been the victim of tiny, inquisitive hands? A very young child, not yet walking, is keen on wanting to grab any object of interest. There is no fault in this, but sometimes it can be annoying. When you are holding a baby and he keeps pulling off your glasses, you cannot explain to him the impropriety of such socially impolite behavior. The little tot is not yet moved by social concerns. So do you try to restrain him from getting to your face? No, you train him not to touch. Once you train an infant to respond to the command "No," then you will have control in every area of behavior where you can give a command.

Just as God did in the garden, set up training situations. For example, using your glasses as bait, place the child where he can easily reach them (*"in the midst of the garden"*). Look him squarely in the eye. When he reaches out to grab them, don't pull back; don't defend yourself. Calmly say, "No." Although the "No" should carry a tone of firmness and finality, don't raise the decibel level. Remember, you are establishing a vocal pattern to be used the rest of his youth. If he reaches out to touch your glasses, again say, "No," and thump or swat his hand with a light object so as to cause him a little pain, but not enough to make him cry. He will pull his hand back and try to comprehend the association of grabbing the glasses with the pain. Inevitably, he will return to the bait to test his new theory. Sure enough, reaching for the glasses again causes pain, and the pain is accompanied by a quiet, little "No." It may take one or two more tries for him to give up his career as a glasses snatcher, but he will. Through this process, the child will associate the pain with the word "No." There quickly comes a time when your word alone is sufficient to gain obedience across the board in all situations.

There are many things you can teach the small child at this young age. You can stop him from assaulting his mother with a bottle held by the nipple. The same holds true for hair and beard pulling. You name it, the infant can be trained to obey. Do you want to wrestle with him through his entire youth, nagging him into compliance, threatening, placing things out of reach, fearing what he might get into next? I know a mother who must call a babysitter every time she takes a shower. If your child is four or five years old, you should be able to take a nap and expect to find the house in order when you awake. Wouldn't it be better to take a little time to train him in his young and tender years? If nothing else, training will result in saving you time. **But the fact is, a well-trained child is a happy child.**

OBEDIENCE TRAINING—*BITING BABIES*

One particularly painful experience of nursing mothers is the biting baby. My wife did not waste time finding a cure. Her grandmother and some of the "old timers" informed her of the traditional approach. When the baby bites, gently pull his hair. The baby learns not to bite his mother through the negative consequences associated with it. An alternative has to be sought for bald-headed babies. Understand, the baby is not being punished, just conditioned. A baby learns not to stick his finger in his eyes or bite his tongue through the negative sensation associated with it. Conditioning requires no understanding or reasoning. Somewhere in the brain that information is unconsciously stored. After biting two or three times and experiencing pain in association with each bite, the child stores that information away for his own comfort. The biting "habit" is cured before it starts. This is not discipline. It is obedience training.

OBEDIENCE TRAINING—*BOWLS AND BABIES*

A mother clumsily holds her cereal bowl at arm's length as she wrestles her infant for supremacy. When she places the bowl out of the baby's reach, he is led to believe that the only objects that are off limits are those that are out of reach. To train him, place the bowl within easy reach. When he reaches for it, say, "No," and thump his hand. He will pull his hand back, momentarily look alarmed, and then reach again. Repeat the action of saying, "No" in a calm voice and thumping his hand. After several times you will be able to eat in peace.

After two or three occasions of responding to a thump and the word "No," the voice command alone becomes sufficient to direct the child's behavior. Always keep in mind that the baby is not being punished, just conditioned. The thump is not a substitute spanking. It is reinforcing obedience training.

COME WHEN I CALL YOU

One military father tells of his training sessions with each new toddler. He designates an evening for "booty" camp, which is a boot camp for toddlers. He allows a ten-month-old child to become deeply interested in a toy or some delightful object. From across the room or just inside another room, the father calls the child. If the child ignores the call, the father goes to him and explains the necessity of immediately coming when called, and then leads him through the steps of obedience by walking him over to the place from which he was called. Father then returns him to the toy and leaves him alone long enough to again become engrossed. Father calls again. If the child ignores the call, the father gives additional explanation and a repeat of the practiced walk. The parent, having assured himself that the child understands what is expected of him, goes back to call again. When you first commence training to come on command, it is helpful to reward the child for coming—a hug, bounce in the air, words of praise, etc. This is completely effective.

But once the child fully understands the need to come when called and has willingly responded to the summons many times, there will come a time when he *decides* not to come. Take note of the word *decides*. We are not talking about a situation where the child is distracted or fails to understand what is expected. If that is the case, more walk-through sessions will be in order. However, if the child is indeed rebelling—choosing his own way contrary to the father's command—then while calling him, administer one or two swats with a switch or light instrument on the arm or exposed leg and then continue the exercise until the child readily responds to the summons. Thereafter, until the day the grown child leaves home, you can expect him to drop everything and come when called. *As long as you remain consistent, the child will consistently obey.* This obedience training is conducted with quiet patience. If you are doing it correctly, the child will be trained in a matter of minutes. The swats do not rise to the level of a spanking; they are not punishment and not very painful. They merely focus his attention and give weight to your words.

NEVER TOO YOUNG TO TRAIN

A newborn soon needs training. But parents who put off training until their child is old enough to discuss issues or receive explanations will discover they have a terrorist in the home long before he is big enough to tie his shoes.

As a mother begins to lower her child into the crib, he stiffens, takes a deep breath, and bellows. The battle for control has begun in earnest. Someone is going to be conditioned. Either the tenderhearted mother will cave in to the child's self-centered demands (actually training the child to get his way by crying), or she will wisely ignore the crying (communicating that crying is counterproductive). Crying because of genuine physical need is the infant's only voice to the outside world and should be considered a legitimate voice, but **crying in order to manipulate others into constant servitude should never be rewarded.** Otherwise, you will reinforce the child's growing self-centeredness, which will eventually become socially intolerable. Self-centered, manipulative children and adults are very unhappy and tend toward emotional illness. You can stop it before it happens.

STEPS TO OBEDIENCE

One of our girls, Shalom, who developed mobility early, had a fascination with crawling up stairs. At five months of age she was too unknowing to be punished for disobedience. But for her own good (and our peace of mind), we attempted to train her not to climb the stairs by coordinating the voice command of "No" with little spats on her bare legs. The switch was a twelve-inch-long, one-eighth-inch-diameter sprig from a willow tree. After the command and the switch, she backed off and ceased her effort to climb. She understood quite well the meaning of "No" and the accompanying swat. But such was her fascination with climbing, that after a while she returned to climb again, forgetting the taps with the little switch. Negative consequences are supposed to work, but it seemed that, at her young age, her little brain could not maintain the association. So, out of desperation, and taking my own advice not to continue to spank if it doesn't work, I laid the switch on the bottom step. We later observed her crawl to the stairs and start the ascent, only to halt at the first step and stare at the switch. She backed off and never again attempted to climb the stairs, even after the switch was removed several days later. At the sight of the switch she made the association between the command and the little sting of the switch and decided to refrain from participating in her favorite extreme sport. I had communicated to her my will and my resolve. Keep in mind I was not actually spanking a five-month-old. When children are too young to reason and reflect, spanking is completely inappropriate. The use of the little switch was conditioning, as when a horse trainer pops a whip behind a horse or swings a rope to solicit a response.

TRAINING THE ORNERY AMISH BOY

One cold winter day as I sat talking with a local Amish fellow, a typical child training session developed. The twelve-month-old boy sitting on his father's lap suddenly developed a compulsion to slide to the floor. Wanting to keep the child off of the cold floor, the father directed him to remain seated. The little guy stiffened and threw his arms up to lessen the father's grip so as to facilitate his slide to the floor. The father spoke to him in the German language (which I did not understand) and firmly placed him back in the sitting position. The child made dissenting noises and continued his attempt to dismount his father's lap. The father then swatted the child's leg one time and spoke what I assumed to be reproving words. Seeing his mother across the room, the child began to cry and reach for her. This was understandable in any language. It was obvious the little fellow thought there would be more liberty with his mother.

At this point, I became highly interested in the proceedings. This one-year-old child was attempting to go around the chain of command! Most fathers would have been glad to pass the "troublesome" child to his mother. If the little fellow had been permitted to initiate the transfer, he would have been the one doing the training, not the father. Mothers often run to their children in this situation because they enjoy the feeling of being needed. But this wise mother was more concerned that her child be properly trained than she was with satisfying her own need. She appeared not to hear the child's plea.

The father then turned the struggling child to face away from his mother. The determined fellow immediately understood that the battle lines had been drawn. He expressed his will to dominate by throwing his leg back over to the other side to face his mother. The father swatted the leg the child turned toward his mother and again spoke to him.

Now the battle was in full array. Someone was going to submit his will to the other. Either the father would confirm that this strapping one-year-old could rule his parents, or the parents would confirm their authority. Everyone's happiness was at stake—as well as the character of the child. The father was wise enough to know this was a unique test of authority, something that may happen only once or twice in the life of a child. This episode that began as obedience training had evolved into attitude training.

During the following forty-five minutes as we continued to talk, the child shifted his legs fifteen times and received a swat on the leg each time. The father was as calm as a lazy porch swing on a Sunday afternoon. There was no hastiness or anger in his response. He did not take the disobedience personally. He had trained many horses and mules and knew the value of patient perseverance. In the end, the boy submitted his will to his father, sat as he was placed, and became content—even cheerful. He was now ready to quietly sit through three hours of the most boring church service a sleeping patriarch ever attended.

Some will say, "But I couldn't take it emotionally." Sometimes it *is* difficult to set aside your feelings for the sake of training your children. It does involve emotional sacrifice. Yet, what is love but giving? When we know it will work to the temporal and eternal good of our children, it becomes a joy instead of a sacrifice. It is a thrill to see it work to the child's benefit.

If you know you are prone to anger or impatience, it will deter you from being active in disciplining your child. You may fear that your discipline is an act of your ego to dominate. If that be true, then you must first deal with your own hang-ups for the sake of the child; for if he doesn't receive consistent training he will greatly suffer later in life.

BE ASSURED OF TWO THINGS

First, the best-trained child will have at least one time in his young life when he will rebel against authority and attempt to take control of the reins as did the Amish kid. This act of stubbornness is profound—amazing—a wonder that one so young could be so dedicated and perseverant in defiance. It is the kind of determination you would expect to find in a hardened revolutionary facing enemy indoctrination. Parents who are trained to expect it and are prepared to stand fast will still be awed at the strength of the small child's will.

Second, if you are consistent in training, this attempt at total dominance may come only once in a child's life, usually around two years old. If you win the first confrontation, the child wins at the game of character development. If you weaken and allow the child to rule, the child loses everything but his will to dominate. You must persevere for the sake of the child. His will to dominate must be dominated by the rule of law that you represent.

You must be consistent if you are to achieve positive results. The cat that is prevented from coming into the house most of the time but is allowed to occasionally break through the barrier to discover some pleasure will take the occasional success as impetus to always try to get in. However, if he is consistently kept out (100% of the time), he will lose the will to come in even when the door is left open. You may scream at him, slam the door on his tail, and kick him sixty feet, but if you occasionally allow him to stay in long enough to eat scraps off the floor or sleep on the couch, he will forever risk running the gauntlet to get in. Your abuse (they mistakenly call it *discipline* where children are involved) may make him sufficiently wary to obey while you remain on guard, but the hairy fur-ball will still bolt through the door when he sees the opportunity.

On the other hand, dogs, many times smarter than cats, can be trained either to come in or stay out on command. The key is always consistency. If Rover learns through conditioning (consistent behavior on the part of the trainer) that he will never be allowed to violate his master's command, he will always obey. If parents carefully and consistently train up their children, their performance will be superior to that of a well-trained, seeing-eye dog.

NEGATIVE TRAINING

How many times have you observed untrained children in the grocery store? A devious little kid sits up in the command seat of the shopping cart exercising his "childhood rights" to unlimited self-indulgence. The parent fearfully but hopelessly steers around the tempting "trees of knowledge of good and evil." Too late! The child spies the colorful object of his unbridled lust. The battle is on. The child will either get what he wants or make his parents miserable. Either way, he conquers.

PURCHASED COMPLIANCE

One father proudly told of how he shrewdly overcame by promising the child a reward of ice cream if he would only wait until they left the store. Such compromises will only affirm the child in his commitment to terrorist tactics. You are not gaining control of the child; he is gaining control of you. **All children are trained, some carelessly or negligently, and some with varied degrees of forethought.** All parental responses are conditioning the child's behavior and are therefore training.

Parents who purchase compliance through promise of reward are turning their child into a racketeer, paying him for protection. The child becomes the Mafia or union boss, and you take the role of intimidated businessman. If you are bargaining with a terrorist for one more day's reprieve from anguish, you may indeed strike a favorable deal. But if you are training up a child, you need to reconsider your methods. Allowing yourself to be manipulated into compromise will turn your child into an intimidating bully.

DID YOU HEAR WHAT I SAID?

I observed a father tell his small boy not to touch a particular object. Having been inadvertently trained to ignore mild commands, the child picked it up anyway. With irritation in his voice, the father demanded, "Give it to me." The boy pretended not to hear. With anger, "Did you hear me? [Of course he did.] Hand it to Daddy." With mounting anger, "Johnnnieee, give it to Daddy, NOW!!" Finally, another decibel higher—hasty—angry—threatening, "JOHNNY!! Am I going to have to SPANK YOU?" By this time the father was aware of his embarrassing tone. He calmed his voice and, in an attempt to bring it to a conclusion, he leaned way out and extended his hand, making it easier for Johnny to comply. Because of his father's angry voice and burning eyes, Johnny assumed the temporary posture of, "Oh well, there will be another day." But instead of handing the object to the humbled, groping father, he held it in his general direction but down close to his body, forcing the father to advance even farther to retrieve it. The father, looking like a poor peasant receiving alms from some condescending member of royalty, submitted to the child's humiliating gesture and reached to retrieve the object. And then, in a final display of weakness, the father placed it out of the child's reach.

What did Johnny learn from this episode? He had his conviction reinforced that it is never necessary to obey a command the first, second, third, or even fourth time. No one expects him to. He has learned that it is permissible to grab anything within reach and to continue possessing it until the heat gets too great. He has learned not to respect authority, just strength (the day will come when he will be the stronger one). By the father's example, he has learned how to use anger. By the father's advance to take the object from his hand, he has learned how to get in the last shot and maintain his defiance. That father was effectively training his small child to be a rebel.

What has the father learned? He has learned that little Johnny is just a "strong-willed" child; that children go through unpleasant "stages"; that it is sometimes a very miserable and embarrassing thing to be a parent; that one has to watch a kid every minute and keep things out of his reach; that the only things kids understand are force and anger—all of which are false. The father is reaping nothing less than the harvest of his failure to train.

CHAPTER 2

Childish Nature
(Understanding a Child's Natural Development)

"BEHOLD, THE SECOND WOE"!

Just last night while sitting in a meeting, I looked over to see a young mother struggling with her small child. He seemed determined to make her life as miserable as possible—and to destroy her reputation in the process. She had the "Why me?" look on her tired face. He kept defiantly throwing his bottle on the floor (encouraged by her picking it up and handing it back to him) and making angry noises that forced the preacher to speak louder and louder. By increasing his embarrassing displays, the child forced her to put him down on the floor. He then proceeded to act as a circus clown, drawing attention away from the preacher. Finally he insisted on procuring a neighbor's property. When the frazzled mother tried to prevent his thievery and rescue the stolen goods, he kicked his legs like an eggbeater, all the while screaming in protest.

It was enough to make you believe the Devil started out as an infant. I am just thankful that one-year-olds don't weigh two hundred pounds, or a lot more mothers would be victims of infant "momicide." It causes one to understand where the concept of a "sinful nature" originated.

The mother knew that the child shouldn't be acting like this, but due to his limited intellectual development she felt helpless. Older children and adults are constrained by public opinion from such embarrassing displays, but children are not affected by peer pressure, threat of embarrassment, or rejection. This little fellow's life was one of unlimited, unrestrained self-indulgence. No doubt, as is usually the case, his parents were waiting for his understanding to develop so they could begin to correct "bad" behavior. They helplessly watched while selfishness and meanness of spirit took root in a void of understanding.

What is the driving force in this child, and how can it be conquered? We need to understand some things about the nature of a child in order to institute appropriate training.

GOD-GIVEN SELF-CENTEREDNESS

God created us to exist in a constant state of desire and appetite. The tension in this struggle between flesh and spirit provides the context for moral development. This is most apparent in the small child. He desires food, water, warmth, companionship, entertainment, and a dry diaper. God endowed him with strong compulsions to taste, smell, hear, and see, and a desire to touch and feel everything.

The desires and passions in the infant are not yet mature. As he ages, he will find himself possessed of ever-increasing, natural desires for things *"pleasant to the eyes,"* things *"good for food,"* and for those things that will *"make one wise"* (Gen. 3:6). His growing humanity will give way to a desire to build, to know, to be appreciated, to be recognized, to succeed, to be a lover, and to survive in a secure state of being.

As infants grow they learn to manipulate their surroundings for their own gratification. A smile, grunt, kicking of the feet, rolling and shaking the head, crying, and screaming all say, "Pick me up, feed me, look at me; doesn't anyone realize I have urgent needs? What could be more important than me?"

An infant's world is no bigger than his needs and desires. Gratification is the only reality he knows. He soon learns that not only can he get his needs satisfied, but his wants as well. The infant cannot think in terms of duty, responsibility, or moral choice. He has no pride or humility—only desire. Like Julius Caesar, he comes, he sees, he conquers. He is created that way. By nature, he is incapable of considering the needs of others. The child doesn't know or care that you are tired and also in need of comfort.

Because of its resemblance to adult behavior, the self-centeredness of infants has all the appearances of a vice. But their actions spring from the natural, God-given impulse of self-interest. They come into the world totally dependent—with many appetites. In an effort to satisfy those appetites they *"go astray as soon as they be born, speaking lies"* (Psalm 58:3). Before they can talk, they learn to lie to their parents by pretending that their wants are really needs. Parents, not being able to discern the difference, rush to serve them, and the child's selfishness grows. Children do not have the intellectual and moral capacity to say "no" to appetites and impulses. They cannot yet be held responsible. They begin life in innocent self-centeredness. God does not impute it to them as sin, but it is the foundation out of which sin will grow.

TO BLAME OR NOT TO BLAME

As the child gets older, say from eight to twelve months, the adults in his life begin to recognize some of the child's behavior as selfishness and respond by paying less attention to his demands. A weaning process begins. The child is made to wait, told "no," and given boundaries. He must learn that he cannot always be first. If early training has not subdued the manifestations of his selfishness, people begin to refer to him as "spoiled."

Guilty, frustrated parents are manipulated by the child's whining and crying. The spatting begins. The kid gets jerked around. Resentment builds. Adults begin to blame him, even compete with him.

The child feels this tension but doesn't understand what has caused it, but neither does he lessen his demands. He connives, calculates, and resorts to angry tantrums. I have seen a two-year-old take a weapon and angrily strike his mother. The young child has not matured to a point where he can understand responsibility, weigh values, and make conscious decisions based on moral or social worth, but he certainly can mimic the criminal mind.

TOWARD UNDERSTANDING

What is happening? A short time ago the adults around this child would have given him anything he wanted, including their own life-sustaining food. Now they are beginning to expect a little giving on his part. But he doesn't want to give. Taking has been his way of life from conception. And this arrangement suits him just fine.

We adults, sensing the capabilities of children, expect them to give and take at a level appropriate to their maturity. When they fall behind our expectations, we become frustrated and then irritated. Children NEVER make a voluntary transition from the utterly dependent and self-centered state to the socially conscious, give-and-take state.

We are delighted when the three-month-old grabs food from our hand and stuffs it into his mouth, but let a three-year-old try it and it is not so cute. We are delighted when a three-year-old interrupts our conversation with a tale of his own, but a nine-year-old is expected to say, "Excuse me," and wait for an appropriate time to participate in the conversation.

When we believe that a child has matured to the point of being capable of responsible action, we automatically expect it of him. However, if he is slow to assume his duty we become irritated with him for not "acting his age."

The beasts of the earth, in contrast to man, never need to deny their natural drives. They are within their intended boundaries when living for self-gratification. But the growing child or adult who doesn't rise above self-indulging desires has fallen from God's intention and design. **The root of all vice is found in the runaway indulgence of God-given desires,** as was the case with Adam and Eve. Although the child may not have matured to the point of accountability, still, his unrestrained indulgence is the very essence of future sinfulness.

A SPIRITUAL FETUS

Life is designed by God to be a spiritual womb, a place where moral development is the product of passions confronted by free choice, and the battle continues throughout life. The early years after birth could be viewed as the prenatal development of a moral being.

At their creation, Adam and Eve were physically complete but morally undeveloped. A four-month fetus, still in the mother's womb, is a living soul. Though all of its tiny members match those of a mature adult, it is yet an incomplete creation, needing further growth before becoming distinct from its mother. In like manner, a three-year-old child, in its soul, has all the tiny features of a morally responsible adult—a knowledge of right and wrong, a sense of justice, accountability, conscience, duty, guilt, shame, etc. Yet none of the moral faculties are developed to the point of being fully operative and independent. The child is not a morally viable soul. He is an incomplete moral being. He is not accountable. Morally, the three-year-old is still in the womb. Moral life begins its development sometime after birth, probably in the second year, and continues until it matures at about ten to fifteen years of age, possibly later.

WHEN DRIVES BECOME SIN

When does this innocent, natural selfishness of a child become sin? In other words, when is a child to blame? There are vast differences of opinion on this subject. From time immemorial, age twelve has been the traditional "age of accountability." But accountability is not an age; it is a state of consciousness (James 4:17; Lev. 5:3). Biblically, it will be sometime before nineteen years of age (Deut. 1:39 with Num. 14:29–31).

Observation seems to suggest that some children may be accountable as early as five, while others may not be fully accountable until eighteen. The mentally impaired may never develop to the point of moral responsibility. But again, age is not the issue. The primary issue is that moral development is a process, and the small child is not yet a viable moral soul. All child training must be conducted with this firmly in mind and must constantly adapt to the progressive moral development of the child.

Like physical development in the womb, moral development is a slow transition from no moral understanding at birth to complete accountability at some point in adolescence. As the child's reason and moral faculties develop, he gradually understands his moral responsibility and duty. At some point (as moral perception grows to a point where he can be held fully accountable), every child faces his own *"tree of the knowledge of good and evil"* (See Deut. 1:39). So far, everyone (except Jesus) has "eaten" (personally violated his own God-given understanding of right and wrong), resulting in personal condemnation.

Again, though the child may feel guilt in some areas, the responsibility for sin is not imputed unto him until his moral soul is fully functional. An unfinished clock, still in the making, may have moving parts, but it will not keep time until every last piece is properly installed.

THE DILEMMA

The dilemma parents face is this: How do we relate to the child during this transitional period as he progresses from no moral understanding to complete accountability? For example, when a five-year-old child is, say, 30% morally cognizant and 70% morally naïve, how does a parent hold the child accountable? We know that God will not condemn a child whose moral faculties are not completely operative, but how do parents determine the degree to which the child should be held responsible? This uncertainty causes many parents to hesitate and postpone the training of their children. But if parents wait until the child can understand the need to exercise self-control before they demand it of him, he will have developed both a history and a habit of indulging his flesh to the fullest. The issue parents must always address is that natural drives are active long before reason awakens. During the years before the child is capable of self-motivated restraint, parents thoughtlessly assist the child's self-indulgence by providing an environment where little is expected.

PARENTAL RESPONSIBILITY

Now we come to the crux of this chapter and the background for this book. It is critically important to understand: **FROM BIRTH, PARENTS MUST ASSUME RESPONSIBILITY FOR THE MORAL DEVELOPMENT OF THEIR CHILDREN.** During the early years, we certainly do not want to destroy the child's natural drives, but we must constrain him to exercise temperance and self-control. A parent's role is not that of policeman but more like that of the Holy Spirit. When a child has his sails full of wind (strong drives), but has no compass (moral discernment), the parent must serve as his compass and navigator. When a child is incapable of holding moral values, parental training and example will be his standard. **Before he can DECIDE to do good, parents must DIRECT him to do good.** There was a time in the womb when the child's mother breathed for him, ate for him, and possessed his waste. Likewise, in the moral realm, until the child's reason and moral faculties develop to the point of independent operation, parents must be the voice of his fetal conscience, providing initiative and instilling values.

Each day brings the child closer to moral responsibility. Someday his spiritual heart will function without you. He will leave the protection of your sanctification and stand alone in the light of his own conscience (1 Cor. 7:14). Until he matures to that point, **the only moderation the child will know is what his parents instill in him by training.**

Parents must be sensitive to their role in the child's moral development. One day he is going to choose without you. Will he make the right choice? No amount of training is going to override the certainty of sin developing in the child's life, but wise parental oversight can lessen the child's addiction to the flesh and make it easier for repentance to follow his sinful indulgence.

You should not deal with the small child's selfishness as sin, but you must be aware that it will soon move in that direction. Drives which are not in themselves evil, nonetheless, form the foundation on which sin will assuredly grow. As you train your young child, you must take into consideration the evil that a self-willed spirit will eventually bring.

You cannot impart righteousness to your children, but you can help them develop a firm commitment to righteousness. You cannot write the law on their hearts, but you can weave the law and the gospel into their developing consciences (2 Tim. 3:15).

Anticipating the child's development and knowing that evil will come to be a part of his moral being places an urgent sense of responsibility upon parents. The world is a powerful, unrelenting undertow pulling children to destruction. Looking at statistics alone, the probability is overwhelmingly against their moral survival. The training you give and the wisdom you impart can make all the difference in the outcome. You hold an eternal soul in your hands. You cannot afford to give in to weariness, indifference, laziness, or careless neglect. God chose you two as the parents of these children! It is now your responsibility to determine what level of understanding your child possesses and to hold him accountable at that level.

This is an almost impossible task if you depend on your intellect alone. As the principal caretaker of your child, your heart will be able to discern the world from his perspective. When the child believes it is wrong, it is wrong (James 4:17). Where the child possesses moral understanding yet willfully disobeys, he should be rebuked, instructed, and chastened if needed. Where he does not understand the moral quality of his actions he should be trained and conditioned.

WALKING AFTER THE FLESH

All children seem bent toward selfish gratification. This propensity originates in the fleshly body seeking pleasure. After the child has given himself over to fleshly appetite, Paul labels his flesh as *"sinful flesh"* (Rom. 8:3), that is, flesh full of sin. Sinful flesh is not sinfulness of the substance of flesh, rather sinfulness of the person who walks after the flesh. As the body of flesh was the medium of Eve's sin and of Christ's temptation, so it is the implement of your child's development into selfishness—which, at maturity, will constitute sin-fullness.

WALKING AFTER THE SPIRIT

Even before a child's conscience begins to operate, you must train him to practice self-restraint. For if a child is allowed to violate his budding conscience, and continues to do so as he grows to full maturity, he will find himself already fully given over to his flesh long before he begins to develop a sense of duty. Therefore, before moral development even begins (at about two years of age), parents must direct the child to bring his flesh into complete subjection to the principles of righteousness (the rule of law).

By the third year and beyond, that part of the child that is awakened to moral duty should be taught to voluntarily surrender to the rule of law. If you allow the flesh to run its natural course, the child will be possessed of many unruly passions and lusts long before he is cognizant enough to assume responsibility.

IN MY HANDS

The clay formed into a vessel of dishonor was marred while in the potter's hand, only to be remade into a vessel of honor fit for the master's table. If God is the potter and your child is the clay, you are the wheel on which the clay is to be turned. As Adam and Eve were given a garden to dress and keep, you have been given loan of a little heart and mind to dress and keep.

There will come a time when your child must stand alone before *"the tree of the knowledge of good and evil."* As the purpose of God has permitted, he will inevitably partake of the forbidden fruit. Now, in the developing years, you can make a difference in how he will respond after he has "eaten." Will he opt for Adam and Eve's fig-leaf coverings or for God's sacrificial covering? Will he hide his sin or repent?

Everything a child experiences, either by way of indulgence or the self-restraint you impose upon him, is preparing him for the day when he will mature into a responsible, moral soul. Somewhere on that road of development, each child will graduate into a state of full accountability. That child then stands alone before God *"without excuse."* That moment becomes his day of *accountability*.

A DIVINE CALLING

With this understanding, you can better appreciate what is taking place in your developing child. Just as the child Jesus *"increased in wisdom and stature, and in favour with God and man"* (Luke 2:52), so your child is going to experience a growth of understanding. God's grace reaches out through the Holy Scriptures which are able to make him *"wise unto salvation"* (2 Tim. 3:15). You, the parents, must equip your child to save himself from this *"untoward generation"* (Acts 2:40). God already has a prototype of the finished child: It is that he might be *"conformed to the image of his Son"* (Rom. 8:29), which can only be realized when he is born again. But you can work with God toward the day when your child will be conformed to *"the measure of the stature of the fulness of Christ"* (Eph. 4:13). The promise of God is still operative: *"Train up a child in the way he should go: and when he is old, he will not depart from it"* (Prov. 22:6). **You can begin the child's sanctification long before his salvation.** Why let him develop hang-ups that will be a drag on him after he is born again?

CHAPTER 3

Parental Anger

NO MORE CHANCES

As I was working on this book, a young mother said to me, "I get so angry sometimes; I treat the children so badly. They just constantly upset me. Johnny is always picking on Mary and making her whine. I have to just stay on top of them all the time to prevent them from doing something they shouldn't. What can I do to overcome my anger?"

She had been responding to their disobedience by saying, "Now, Johnny, I have told you not to do that. I am going to give you one more chance and then I will have to spank you." As he continued to disobey, her frustration mounted and she gave him another chance . . . and another. By her empty threats she had effectively taught Johnny that he could disobey until her frustration boiled over into near rage. When he suspected she was near the breaking point, he would back off and "obey" for a while. He knew he could return to unhindered self-will as soon as she cooled off. Sometimes, miscalculating, he pushed her too far and she would "explode" before he could comply. He had learned to "work" his mother, but she was so inconsistent that he sometimes miscalculated and got into trouble. Admittedly, it is often difficult for a small child to train his mother without her complaining.

In time, she always got him to obey, usually after a long, tense confrontation. The kid was responding quite predictably. She had trained him not to obey until her anger reached a certain intensity. They had something in common—consistency. He was consistent, and she was consistently inconsistent.

31

I gave her a copy of this manuscript in its early form. After reading it, she decided to make some changes at home. She made it plain to her son that he was not to tease his smaller sister. She told Johnny that if he disobeyed, he would be spanked for the first offense. The first spanking was a shock to Johnny. Mother was no longer waiting until she got mad. No warnings, no threats. She expected him to obey—the very first time!

After two days of Mother rewarding every transgression with a spanking, Johnny turned to her and said, "But Mother, you are not giving me any more chances!" The mother said, "That's right, you don't get any more chances. From now on I will expect you to obey the first time." He had been using his chances to purchase disobedience. Two years later, he continues to obey the first time, and Mother has continued in a state of peace without getting angry. Obviously, they are both happier with the new arrangement.

LICENSE TO DISOBEY

When the State Fish & Game Commission issues permits allowing you to catch seven trout and no more, they are not preventing trout fishing, they are advocating it. This mother had issued Johnny a license to be disobedient seven times, but only chastened him for the last offense. So every day he went fishing for trouble, but always with an eye on the "warden." He would try to anticipate when to stop short of the real "last chance."

When Mom outlawed disobedience by reducing the "limit" to zero, little Johnny had to test the lawgiver to see if it was just another "permit." When Mother Warden proved to be serious, he decided that he didn't love fishing for trouble enough to pay the fine for what he caught. Little Johnny started obeying all laws—the first time.

If state troopers ceased writing speeding tickets and instead started nagging and threatening, it would be tantamount to abolishing the speed limit. Picture a trooper pulling a speeder over and then explaining how sad it makes him feel for them to be going so fast. Can you see a trooper sitting on the side of the road shaking his fist and turning red in the face as each car speeds by? Imagine him pulling a speeder over for the sixth time and saying, "Now, I am not going to tell you again!" If this were the case, then all law and order would break down into *"every man did that which was right in his own eyes"* (Judges 21:25). Sounds like the average family, doesn't it?

Most automobile drivers are aware that the radar patrolman will usually allow motorists to go four miles-per-hour over the speed limit without issuing a ticket. Consequently, most motorists will drive four or five miles-per-hour over the speed limit *without fear!* When you allow your children to be disobedient four or five times before applying discipline, you are *training* them to disobey eighty percent of the time.

Parent, you can't blame your children if you have trained them to delay obedience until after several warnings, threats, an ultimatum or two, and anger, followed with a display of force. It's not their fault. *It's yours.*

UGLY ANGER

Parent, have you developed the habit of not disciplining immediately, but waiting until your irritation builds into anger? If so, then you have allowed anger to become your inducement to discipline—a less-than-worthy motivation—actually a selfish motivation. "But how can I stop being so angry?" you ask. It's simple. Your anger comes from your frustration. So don't wait until the child's disobedience becomes a personal affront to you. Discipline (not necessarily spank) immediately upon the slightest disobedience. When children see you motivated by anger and frustration, they assume that your "discipline" is just a personal matter, a competition of interests. The child thinks of you much as he would of any other child who is bullying him around. He is not being made to respect the law and the lawgiver. He believes that you are forcing him to give in to superior power. When you act in anger, your child feels that you are committing a personal transgression against him—violating his rights. In so doing, you have lost the dignity of your office. As politicians often say, "You are not presidential enough." If your child does not see consistency in the lawgiver, in his mind there is no law at all, just competition for supremacy.

You have taught yourself to be motivated only by anger. And you have taught your child to respond only to anger. Having failed to properly train your child, you have allowed the seeds of self-indulgence and rebellion to grow to ugly proportions.

I MADE A CHILD THAT I DON'T LIKE

The reason you are angry toward your child is that you don't like him. "Oh! I love my child very much!" I didn't say you don't love him. I said, there are occasions when you just don't like him, for the simple reason that at such times he is indeed very unlikable. It is impossible to like a whining, selfish, self-centered, spoiled brat. But then, you know that you are guilty of training him to be that way. We cannot help approving of that which is good and lovely and despising that which is ugly and unwholesome, even when we see it in our own flesh and blood. God Himself has such feelings (see Psalm 11:5).

You must face the fact that there are times when you just do not like your own child, and for good reasons. Many times I have observed parents expressing what could only be called "intense dislike" for their teenage son or daughter. You may say, "But no one else seems to dislike them." They would if they had to share the same house or a long drive in the car.

But again I ask: Why is your child unlikable? You may not like the answer: You made him that way through your training techniques. You may say, "But I have not instituted any training techniques. I just scold him when it gets to be too much to bear." Precisely! All children are trained by the responses and actions—or the lack thereof—of their principal caretakers. Negative training at its best—or should I say, worst—is done by those who, while failing to properly train, try to keep their children in line through threat, intimidation, nagging, anger, and an occasional outburst of spanking.

There is nothing cute or lovable about a whining brat. To allow a child to whine and disobey is to mold a personality and character that you and everyone else will find hard to like. By taking control and teaching them to control their emotions and to instantly obey, your children will be cheerful and pleasant. Then you will not only *love* your children but *like* them as well. The child reciprocates the parents' delight by loving and honoring them even more. They can both enjoy each other's company. The parents are rested and refreshed by spending time with their children.

THE FOURTEEN-YEAR-OLD

In talking with a mother concerned about the attitude of her fourteen-year-old daughter, it became apparent that she just did not like her own child. The mother's disapproval and frequent criticism had caused the girl to withdraw and become uncommunicative.

Actually, she was very good and cheerful with others, but sullen with her mother. The mother was wondering if she should use the rod to correct bad attitudes. She was afraid she had lost all control and influence. The mother had a very stormy youth and was anxious to prevent her daughter from suffering the same fate. The more irritated the mother became and the harder she pushed, the more ground she lost. Sometimes in the areas of talent and personality, parents have narrow expectations for their children and are critical when they fail to measure up to their standards.

I knew this family when their daughter was a child. I recall that even then the mother didn't like her. This mother did eventually realize the error of her ways. In taking her own ugly attitude to Christ she found cleansing and healing. Her daughter quickly showed tremendous improvement.

In reality, when parents are poor trainers, they come to dislike the children they have produced. **If you have painted a picture you don't like, don't blame the canvas.** Get out the brushes and paint something better over the mess you made.

CHAPTER 4

Tying Strings

MANY STRINGS MAKE STRONG CORDS

There is a mystical bond between caring members of a loving family. I can look at each of my children and feel that union. It is as if we were joined by many strings of mutual love, respect, honor, and memory of all the good times we've had together.

When two or more people are living together, their interests, opinions, and liberties sometimes clash. Selfishness, indifference, pride, and self-will often cut the strings that unite. When there is not a regular tying of new strings, family members soon find themselves separated by suspicion, distrust, and criticism. The gap can grow so wide that family members become veritable enemies. When this happens between parent and child, it is a serious crisis. Unless new strings are tied, the two will increasingly grow apart. When a teenager says something like, "My parents don't understand me," or "They don't care," it is a sad testimony of an imminent cutting of all strings.

PAPER HEARTS

Recently, a father told us of a victory in this area. His first-grader came home from school and occupied himself drawing and cutting out paper hearts. The father and son were close and often did things together. Yet, in one thoughtless and insensitive moment the father lightly poked fun at his son's activity. The child didn't see anything amusing. He turned away and continued his labor of love. Over the next several days the boy concealed his endeavors from his father. The father became aware that a confidence crisis had occurred. The child was withdrawn and resisted all overtures to fellowship. The strings had been cut.

If, at this point, the father had accepted this wall as nothing more than a "stage"—or worse, had become irritated and contributed further to the breach—this could have been the beginning of a rift that would have grown wider with the years. But the father was wise and took positive action. After school one day, he said to his son, "Hey, Jesse, you want to go out to the shop with me? We will cut out wooden hearts." Jesse looked up and seemed to be cautiously analyzing his father's intent. After a moment his facial expressions changed to believing delight, and he said, "Sure, Dad, that would be great." As they worked together creating a wooden heart for Jesse to give to his friend, the wall came down and their camaraderie was restored.

It is important that sons and daughters be able to trust their parents with personal, intimate knowledge. If there is a barrier in this area, when the time comes that they need intimate counsel, to whom shall they go? The feelings of a child are just as important and sacred as those of an adult—and a lot more fragile. Always treat your children with respect. Never ridicule, mock, or laugh at your child's ideas, creations, or ambitions. The trust you desire to have when they are older must be established and maintained when they are young. If you have an older child with whom you have failed in this area, it is not too late to apologize and reestablish that trust. It may take a while to earn their confidence, but it can be done. God delights in seeing it happen!

CUT STRINGS

I would say that most parents at some time have allowed the strings that unite them to their children to be cut, and they have not made a responsible effort to tie new ones. It is critical that you take care of this issue immediately. When the strings have been cut, all training and discipline will be counterproductive. Without mutual respect and honor, you will only anger and further embitter the child.

I talk with many parents who have lost the respect of their children. For every occasion they tie strings, there are many more occasions they cut the strings of fellowship. Not only is there no longer a bond, but there is a wall between them. The parent takes the child's withdrawal and resentment as rebellion (which it is) and fights back with tongue and rod. Like a wild animal, the child further withdraws into his own safe world of suspicion and distrust.

As a warden can constrain the inmates to compliance, a stern parent can use tongue and rod to force outward compliance, but they will not mold character or tie strings of fellowship. The parent feels the child slipping away, sometimes into the fellowship of bad habits or undesirable company. The parent's anger and rejection will never stitch up the breach. Love and honor cannot be gained through criticism and intimidation.

Another failing approach is to resort to sympathy tactics ("If you loved me," or "You hurt me so much," or "How could you do this to me?") which may elicit token compliance, but will only cause the child to yearn for the day when he or she can get away and be free. By yielding to this tragic, weak-kneed tactic, many parents have driven their young daughters into the arms of an unwholesome lover, or caused their sons to move out.

Parents often develop adversarial relationships with their child, but are not concerned about it because the child doesn't possess the means to manifest his hurt. By the time parents are forced to admit there is a problem, there is a war zone of obstacles between them. What a child is at four, he will be at fourteen, only magnified many times over. Your two-year-old whiner will be a twelve-year-old unthankful grouch. The intemperate five-year-old will be an indulgent fifteen-year-old.

STRINGS LEFT UNTIED

A mother came to us concerned for her fourteen-year-old daughter. She had been reared in a much protected environment and was outwardly obedient, but her parents felt there was a breach in the family ties. When given a chore, the girl would obey but with a sullen attitude. It seemed to this mother that her daughter was tolerating her family but was not at all pleased with their company. There were periods of withdrawal. She seemed to have her own little world. With no outward disobedience, there was nothing for which to reprimand her. This mother had lost fellowship with her daughter. The strings had been cut so long ago that rebuke or discipline would be fruitless, even harmful, until the strings of mutual respect and trust could be retied.

THE THREE-YEAR-OLD TRUCKER

As my wife sat talking to a friend, an altercation developed between the young mother's two sons, ages one and three. They both began to scream while tugging at opposite ends of the same toy truck. The mother hollered, "What is wrong with you two?"

"He is trying to take my truck," cried the older of the two.

"Billy, give Johnny back his truck," she yelled.

After further peace-shattering threats and screams of protest, he reluctantly handed over the truck. The younger child then dejectedly left the yard and stumbled into the house to stand beside his mother—thus punishing the other brother by depriving him of his company. This is an adult form of retribution that children quickly learn.

After the chastisement of loneliness had done its work, the older brother became repentant. Retrieving his truck from the sand pile, he made his way into the house where he found the offended younger brother now sitting in his mother's lap being consoled for his losses on the battlefield. With a smile of reconciliation, the older brother held out the truck to his brother. As the younger brother was about to accept the sacrificial peace offering, the mother turned to see the grinning child dribbling sand from his truck onto the floor. "Get that thing out of here!" she commanded.

The mother was engrossed in her company and failed to regard her children as human beings with complex feelings. She just saw another cleaning job added to her burden.

At this point, a psychological transformation occurred in the child. He had just experienced a "repentance" that had cleansed him of anger and selfishness. Weighing his right to possess the truck against his brother's company, he had found that he valued his brother more. He was learning important social lessons about give and take. He was learning to share and how to control his possessiveness. His heart was surrendered and vulnerable. He had gone the second mile. Yet, when he got to the end of it, he was shocked to find that no one cared. It really didn't matter. He had laid down his guns in surrender, only to be fired upon. If they were not going to allow him to surrender, if they didn't care enough to accept his offering, he was not going to stand there exposed, grinning like a fool, while being unjustly blasted.

He didn't understand what the fray was all about. Who could be upset about a little sand on the floor? After all, he had been playing in sand all morning—he loved it! As he studied his mother's threatening face, you could see the little mental wheels turning. Immediately his smile was replaced by wonder, then puzzlement, and finally, defiance. On his face I saw a devious idea hatched. Knowing that sand on the floor was what stole his show and made her angry, he raised his truck to examine it, and then defiantly dumped the full contents onto the floor. To his satisfaction, it worked. She came apart. She had hurt him, and he had successfully retaliated. "Just look at her red face. That will teach her to attack me. Boy, I won this round."

This mother had missed the opportunity to accept the surrender of this rebel leader. Instead, she had driven him back into the countryside to practice his civil dissent in defiance of the established authority. Like many rebels, he had no alternate plans for the future. He lived to be a rebel because of his hatred for the authority that he hoped to punish for perceived injustices.

Now, you may think that I am over-dramatizing the child's feelings. It is true that he is not consciously thinking such thoughts, but this three-year-old child demonstrated that he had a root of bitterness producing his rebellion.

If the parents don't change, by the time that boy becomes a teenager they will throw up their hands and say, "I don't understand that boy. We have taught him right from wrong, taken him to church, and given him what he wants, but he acts as though we are the enemy. We have done our best. It is up to the good Lord now."

This mother is failing to tie strings of common respect. The seeds sown at three years will bear awful fruit at fourteen.

PROBLEM PARENTS

Parent, if you are having problems with your children, know that they are having problems with you. You are going to have to make adjustments in your own life if you are going to be of any help to them. Since you are the one reading this book, not your children, and since you are the more experienced of the two, and since God didn't say, "Children, train up your parents," the responsibility for making a significant change is completely yours.

CUTTING STRINGS

I still remember looking into the face of one of my boys, knowing that I had cut the strings of trust and fellowship. It was painfully disturbing to see him slip from the moorings I had so carefully built, and now he was drifting away. At the time, I had not yet formulated the terminology for such a problem, nor even recognized the principle, but I could sense that there was a breach. The fault line was widening. And the fault was mine. I had pushed him too hard, demanded too much, and then been critical when he had not performed to my expectations. When, like a turtle, he withdrew into his shell, I could see that he had dismissed me. He had decided to live without me. There was too much pain associated with his father.

I didn't know how to define it, but being fully responsible for his training, I knew that it was my responsibility. I immediately apologized, lightened up, revised my criticism, found the good in what he had done, and suggested an exciting outing. It took me a day or two of being sensible, fair, just, and kind to completely restore the strings of fellowship. He quickly forgave me, and we were restored to comradeship.

GOD HELP THE FATHERS!

"And, ye fathers, provoke not your children to wrath: but bring them up in the nurture and admonition of the Lord" (Eph. 6:4). A father who teases his children until they are angry can expect them to do the same to others smaller than themselves. On more than one occasion when scuffling with my boys, I have found myself having fun at their expense. (That was when I was bigger than they were.) They reminded me to play by the same rules to which they were bound.

Don't shrug this off, fathers. If you make your little boy mad while you are having fun, you are creating either a bully or a broken soul. After all, weren't you really bullying him? The wrath you provoked in him will be stored up until he can release it on someone weaker than himself. That anger can only be put away if he forgives you. And he cannot forgive until he sees your repentance.

If your child shows evidence of a root of bitterness, you have a healing ministry to perform. But first, your heart and life must be fully surrendered to God or you will be wasting your time. In that case, you will just have to try to stay out of his way. He will be rearing himself. His chances are not good, but don't increase his bitterness by playing the hypocrite. It is hard enough to make it in this godless world when you have good support. For a kid filled with bitterness and facing it alone, there is not much hope. Maybe his mother can make a difference. Often a boy just shuts out a father for whom he has only disdain, and so relates to his mother in a manner that may allow him to grow up normal.

Father, if you care for your child's soul more than your pride, then humble yourself and ask his forgiveness (even if he is just two years old). Then, become a patient father and husband. (Your wife will also feel your impatience.) Spend time with your child doing things that are creative—things that give him a sense of great adventure or accomplishment. You can't lead your child closer to God, peace, and discipline than you are yourself.

WHAT CAN I DO NOW?

Start tying some strings. You must be knit together with your child before you can train him. Confess your failure to God and to your child, asking him to forgive you for anger and indifference. At first he will suspect it is just a manipulative ploy on your part and will keep his distance. But when he sees that you are sincere he will respond with forgiveness. Begin the rebuilding process immediately.

Don't barge in and overpower your children with emotion or a new philosophy. Be a friend. Do things with them that they enjoy. Show interest in things that interest them. Be more ready with your ears than with your mouth. Be very sensitive to their concerns. Tie strings until you have earned their respect and honor. If they sense that you like and enjoy them, they will respond in kind. When they like you, they will want to please you and will be open to your discipline.

The strongest cord of discipline is not found in the whip; rather, it is in the weaving together of many strings of mutual love, respect, honor, loyalty, admiration, and caring. It is the difference in being led by the Spirit and being under the works of the law. The law gives us direction, but only the Spirit of grace gives us power. If you will cultivate fellowship with your child, you will have such cooperation and compliance that you will forget where you last left the rod.

WALKING IN MY FATHER'S LIGHT

I can remember an incident that occurred when I was only four years old. Several of us young kids about the same age were walking along behind a row of houses when one of them took his slingshot and shattered a basement window. Through his urging, the other boy also shot out a window. It was my turn. They handed the "weapon" to me. The thought of shooting the slingshot and breaking the glass seemed like such a powerful and thrilling thing to do.

I can still remember my thought process. As I considered shattering the window and readied the slingshot, I visualized my daddy's countenance. He never told me not to break windows, but I knew he wouldn't be pleased. I imagined his sadness and disappointment. I had no law to go by, but I had my father's spirit to guide me. It was not the fear of punishment or scolding that motivated me. It was the fear of losing fellowship with my father that led me in the path of righteousness. To please him and enjoy his favor was my strongest impulse. Walking in my father's light, I handed the slingshot back to the owner and withdrew from the window-breaking party.

My father was not perfect. He wasn't even the best of Christians, but I was not yet aware of that at four, or even at ten years of age. To me, he was law and grace. As I grew older, I slowly (sometimes with a jolt) came to see him as just another struggling member of the human race. Still, I never outgrew that desire to please him.

As I grew older and my dependence on him waned, my confidence in God grew. With the eventual complete transfer of my faith to God (as it should be), I found myself still motivated not by the law and a fear of hell, but by the face of both my father and my Heavenly Father. Today, I have a doubly lighted path.

Parent, above all, you must cultivate this kind of a relationship with your child. It is a painful experience to sin against your best buddy. If you can maintain this kind of bond with your children, you will never have a problem child. Deb and I raised five children, with none of them ever rebelling against our authority.

SEEING GOD IN DADDY AND MAMA

When a child is young, his parents are the only "god" he knows. As he awakens to divine realities, it is through his earthly father that he understands his Heavenly Father. Fathers (and mothers, also), you are the window through which your young child understands God. A child learns the character of God by observing it in his parents. It is not necessary for parents to be perfect, just a balanced representation of God's personality. Within the limits of their humanity parents should emulate the full character and governance of God. Parents need not be all-powerful, just the child's source of strength. They don't have to be all-wise, just wise enough to guide the child and warrant admiration. Parents are not required to be sinless, just demonstrate a commitment to goodness. As a child sees his parents' humble dependence on and love for God, and because he loves and respects them, he will love and honor the One his parents love.

As the child relates to the figurehead of parental authority, in like manner he will later be prone to relate to God. If parents allow their commands to be treated lightly, the child will take the commandments of God lightly also. Children raised by fathers who are permissive and slow to assume command may grow up with no fear of God and no respect for his commandments.

On the other extreme, children with overbearing or cruel fathers usually mature with a foreboding of their Heavenly Father, whereas those made to lovingly obey their earthly fathers are more ready to obey their Heavenly Father.

YOU CAN RE-TIE THE STRINGS

If you sense that the strings of fellowship have been cut, you will want to tie new ones. Here are just a few suggestions on tying strings:

- First and foremost, look at your children with pleasure and smile at them. Bathe them in facial expressions of pleasure and satisfaction.

- Enjoy their company and demonstrate it by inviting them to go with you when the only reason is a desire to have them with you. For the very young, look at pictures or read a book together.

- Sit on the floor and play. Tumble and roll, laugh, and tickle.

- Take them on outings of adventure, excitement, and "danger."

- Take a ten-minute trip to the tree house to see their creations.

- Let them lead you out to the yard to show off their latest stunt.

- Make a kite or build a birdhouse together.

- Mother, teach your children to do everything that must be done in the house. Make it a fun experience. Don't use your children as slave labor or they will experience burnout. Let them bake cookies at two years of age. When you are sewing, let the young ones sit on the floor and cut out doll clothes. When you are painting, let them make a few swipes.

- Fathers, involve your sons in the manly role of protector and provider. If they can walk, they can carry in groceries or bring in firewood. Brag on their achievements.

The idea is for them to feel that they are very special to you and for them to know that you find great satisfaction and delight in sharing with them. If you order your life so your children feel needed, they will desire to walk in harmony with you. Positive words must be in the context of positive participation; otherwise words will lose their meaning and become hollow to the child.

CHAPTER 5

The Rod

Corporal chastisement has been approved and practiced by wise and compassionate men in every culture throughout history. It is mainstream, traditional, grassroots, and effective—a natural part of parental nurturing, of caring parents seeking the best for their children. Hence, it is not surprising to find it promoted by God Himself. *"Chasten thy son while there is hope, and let not thy soul spare for his crying"* (Prov. 19:18).

"I LOVE MY BABY TOO MUCH TO SPANK HIM"

I observed a mother vainly trying to get her discontented child to obey a simple command, but he was too preoccupied with his complaining, whining, and anger. The little tyrant's rebellious antics left the mother miserable and ill-tempered. She continued to plead with him as if she were trying to remember what she had learned about "positive affirmation," not wanting to "stifle his personal expressions." She could have sent him to sit in the corner, but she didn't want the corner damaged.

As an objective observer concerned only for the child's happiness and well-being, I said to the mother, "Why don't you give him a spanking and make him happy?" In shock she replied, "Oh, he will grow out of it. It's just a stage he is going through."

If she truly believes that this is just a natural stage (a condition for which little Johnny is not responsible), why is she provoked to anger, demanding a different conduct or attitude? This mother, while excusing him and maintaining an anxious vigil for the "stage" to run its course, and in spite of her verbalized philosophy to the contrary, does blame the child. Down inside, she knows he should be—could be—decidedly different. The criticism and rejection he feels from his disapproving mother and from the public in general sets him against authority in general. A spanking that would end his bad attitude would be the sensitive, compassionate thing to do. It is abusive to allow the child to continue in that state of contention and frustration, which naturally leads to feelings of rejection.

SPANKINGS

We have progressed to the place where a discussion of the use of the rod is in order. Let's talk about spankings—sometimes called *whippings* down South. The British call it swatting, and that is fine since we all have fly swatters on hand. Corporal chastisement is as traditional as family meals and far more common, practiced by over 90% of parents in the U.S. This is one of the few times God agrees with the 90%. *"He that spareth his rod hateth his son: but he that loveth him chasteneth him betimes"* (Prov. 13:24). *Betimes* doesn't mean "many times"; it means "timely, early." What God says is the exact opposite of the feelings of many parents and progressive academics. The passage clearly states that a failure to apply the rod results in the parents' hating their son. Children that are properly spanked in a context of love and goodwill are purged of their ugliness and become lovely in the sight of adults who then dote on them, brag on what "good kids they are," and take great pleasure in their presence. So which is better: to make them happy with properly ordered discipline or to leave them miserable and rejected with empty threats and criticism?

Those mothers who cry, "But I love my child too much to spank him" do not understand five things: (1) the authority of God's Word, (2) the nature of love, (3) their own feelings, (4) the character of God, and (5) the needs of the child.

1. Understanding the Authority of God's Word

The same God who said: *"Suffer the little children to come unto me, and forbid them not . . ."* (Mark 10:14), also said:

> Chasten thy son while there is hope, and let not thy soul spare for his crying (Prov. 19:18).

> He that spareth his rod hateth his son: but he that loveth him chasteneth him betimes [promptly] (Prov. 13:24).

> Foolishness is bound in the heart of a child; but the rod of correction shall drive it far from him (Prov. 22:15).

Withhold not correction from the child: for if thou beatest him with the rod, he shall not die. Thou shalt beat him with the rod, and shalt deliver his soul from hell (Prov. 23:13–14).

The word *beat* has acquired a different connotation from its usage 400 years ago. It denotes repeated striking as in beating a drum, not as in wounding.

The rod and reproof give wisdom: but a child left to himself bringeth his mother to shame (Prov. 29:15).

Correct thy son, and he shall give thee rest; yea, he shall give delight unto thy soul (Prov. 29:17).

2. Understanding the Nature of Love

You may feel that love prevents you from applying corporal chastisement. But there are millions of parents who testify that love is what motivates them to spank their children, and their children interpret it as love. The God who made little children and therefore knows what is best for them has instructed parents to employ the "rod" in training up their children. To refrain from doing so based on a claim of love is an indictment against God Himself. Your actions declare that God does not desire what is best for your child and you are wiser than is he.

Parent, *you must recognize the difference between true love and sentiment.* Natural human sentiment—often taken to be love—can be harmful if not submitted to wisdom. Love is not sentiment. That is, love is not simply the deep feelings we often have in association with those close to us. Such feelings can be, and often are, self-serving.

Love is not an emotion at all. Love, in the purest sense, is goodwill toward and good doing for others. *"Thou shalt love thy neighbor as thyself."* True love is disinterested. That is, there is no thought of personal gain or of personal loss in the act of loving.

If your early experiences or the examples you have personally witnessed indicate that on the one side is love and on the opposite side is spanking, you are greatly prejudiced by unfortunate experiences that are not the norm.

3. Understanding One's Own Feelings

Mother, if you are emotionally needy, you may look to your child's clinging dependence for personal fulfillment. There is indeed something quite satisfying about being needed by a precious child. It can cause us to dote on the child's every want. No one knows that better than a grandparent. A mother can act too much like a grandmother, afraid to do anything that might cause the child to reject her, avoiding spanking or disciplining while trying to nurse the relationship for all the personal satisfaction it will bring. It feels like love, but it is so adulterated with self-interest that the needs of the child are overlooked. The emotionally needy mother is too pained at the thought of obeying God in employing physical chastisement as part of her child training tools. *"He that spareth his rod hateth his son: but he that loveth him chasteneth him betimes"* (Prov. 13:24).

Again, if you fail to work self-discipline into your child, you will come to "hate" the product of your womb. Blinded by your own need, you convince yourself that your "sweet" child will grow out of it and become a wonderful person. You think, "Just give him more love and a little more time; he doesn't understand yet." *True love is ignoring your needs and doing what is good for the child.* If you should smother your baby while possessively kissing him, you have not loved him no matter how good it felt at the time.

Anger

There are many parents who don't spank, and for good reason. They distrust their motives in corporal chastisement. (See Chapter 3, "PARENTAL ANGER.") Most of those who are spanking abolitionists will immediately launch into a story of how their tyrannical, unreasonable father abused them in the name of spanking. If that is your experience, you may have vowed, "I will never be like my father. I will love my children. They will not fear me the way I feared my father." Your father not only hurt you, he is now hurting your children by causing you to react in the opposite extreme. On the other hand, **if you inherited your father's anger, then by all means do not spank.** But be assured, your words may be equally abusive. There is no alternative to becoming a lovely person, a self-controlled, compassionate parent who proactively trains, maintaining a balanced approach.

One time when I was appearing on a national TV program debating a child psychologist on the subject of spanking, I said, "But we never spank in anger." She almost screamed at me, "But everybody gets angry at their children." It shocked me. Sitting in front of me was a professional psychologist who did not know the world of peace and joy from which I came. In her world, parents could not trust themselves to administer measured discipline to their children. They are handicapped by fear of self. Wow! If it is a justified fear, then what hope is there for their children?

A House Divided

A divided household is destructive to the children. Sometimes a mother's past experience with an angry father will cause her to assume that anyone who spanks a child is angry. She is not in agreement with her husband—the disciplinarian—and their children are well aware of it. When Daddy attempts to discipline them, they flee to Mother for her tender protection. In circumstances like this, the father's discipline will not be effective. The child will grow up with no respect for authority, believing all authority is unjust. Mother, it is time to stop reacting to your past experiences and start acting as God and sound reason dictate.

Peer Pressure

Some parents fail to use the rod because of peer pressure. They may be in disagreement with their own parents about child training. The modern parent is bombarded with propaganda—supposedly based on the latest child development research—that villainizes biblically based (traditional) child rearing. Parents who follow God's pattern of child rearing are "shamed" in modern academia and media, and before applying discipline they must look over their shoulders to see if they are being observed by leftist government goons.

4. Understanding the Character of God

The mother who refrains from the rod based on the excuse that she loves the child too much to spank him does not understand the character and methods of God toward his own people.

There is a twisted perspective that has edged into Christian thinking. It goes something like this: Since God is love, he is not disapproving or censorious in any way. Essentially, they view the love of God as incompatible with the justice of God. It seems to them that he must be either one or the other. There is a vague, undefined sense that God *was* once vengeful in the Old Testament, but is now passive, tolerant, and ecumenical—the Universal Father. God is stripped of his balanced personality and defined in non-threatening ways. Heaven is well received; hell is suspect. *"Judge not,"* the most popular verse in the Bible, is quoted as if God Himself could no longer discriminate between right and wrong.

As much as God is love, he is also holy, just, and true. It is out of his love of righteousness that he is coming in *"flaming fire taking vengeance on them that know not God, and that obey not the gospel of our Lord Jesus Christ"* (2 Thess. 1:8). To choose one side of God's character as a model for our actions while rejecting the other can hardly be called a virtue.

God Spanks His Children

Those who excuse themselves from using the rod by claiming that makes them righteous are, by inference, condemning God. *"For whom the Lord loveth he chasteneth, and scourgeth every son whom he receiveth. If ye endure chastening, God dealeth with you as with sons; for what son is he whom the father chasteneth not? But if ye be without chastisement, whereof all are partakers, then are ye bastards, and not sons"* (Heb. 12:6–8).

The chastisement is represented as a sure sign of love: *"for whom the Lord loveth, he chasteneth."* Then it says he chastens us *"for our profit, that we might be partakers of his holiness"* (Heb. 12:10). This is a most profound statement! God does not have *any* sons who escape chastisement—*"all are partakers."* And did he stop loving those whom he chastened? Quite the contrary, **love was his motivation for the spanking.** Only through chastisement could his sons fully partake of his holiness. *"No chastening for the present seemeth to be joyous, but grievous . . . "* (Heb. 12:11). God's chastisement is a painful experience. Our *"fathers of our flesh . . . chastened us after their own pleasure . . ."* (Heb. 12:9–10). The text speaks positively of our earthly fathers, *"fathers of our flesh,"* chastening their children. God promotes it as a means to holiness—when administered for the son's *"profit."*

If one is not chastened, it is not only an indication of not being loved, but of being a "bastard." The man who has a bastard child in the family may not love him and therefore not stir himself to administer chastisement. The bastard sees the legitimate sons being chastened while he is left to himself. So we see that it is God's love for us, his sons, that motivates his acts of chastisement. Thus, our original passage in Proverbs 13:24 is substantiated: *"He that spareth his rod hateth his son: but he that loveth him chasteneth him betimes."*

If God's love is expressed by his *"grievous"* chastisements, can we not also love our children enough to chasten them unto holiness? I can still remember once hearing a rebellious teenager say, "If they only loved me enough to whip me." What an indictment on his parents!

Recently, a mother told us that after cracking down on her children with consistent use of the rod, one child thanked God for making his mama sweeter. The increased spankings had reduced disobedience, causing the child to be more in harmony with his mother. He interpreted this to be a sweeter mother, **for three spankings a day are much less stressful than fifty scowls and howls of disapproval.** Understand, this mother already had the heart of her children. The only missing element in her parenting was backing up her commands with negative consequences—which sometimes involves the rod. **Keep in mind, no amount of spanking can train a child who does not feel safe and cherished.**

5. Understanding the Needs of the Child

The very nature of the child makes the rod an indispensable element in child training and discipline. We will summarize the previous comments on the nature of a child (Chapter 2) and then draw some important, practical applications.

Summary: *"They go astray as soon as they be born, speaking lies"* (Psalm 58:3). An infant has real needs for food, cuddling, and bodily comfort. But he soon learns that by falsely representing his needs, he can get his *wants* met as well as his needs. He is in the first stages of runaway indulgence. However, due to the immaturity of his soul, God does not count his lies as sin. *"Therefore to him that knoweth to do good, and doeth it not, to him it is sin"* (James 4:17). *"Sin is not imputed when there is no law"* (Rom. 5:13). The infant, not knowing *"good and evil"* (Deut. 1:39), is not held responsible for his lack of conformity to the law. Nevertheless, infants do lie about their condition and needs. And children issue forth with a multitude of other selfishly motivated thoughts and acts that will, upon their growing into the *"knowledge of good and evil,"* constitute a *"body of sin."* Although they are not now to blame, as their moral understanding matures their consciences will be awakened and they will be held accountable.

Your child is in a body of infirm flesh. The God-given drives toward the fulfillment of bodily needs and appetites form a constant and incessant occasion to lust. The drive itself is not sin. Lust of the flesh is natural (Deut. 12:15). But when one is *"drawn away of his own lust, and enticed,"* and the lust conceives with opportunity, *". . . it bringeth forth sin"* (James 1:14–15).

You cannot prevent your child from the trials that his body of flesh will bring, but you can train him in self-denial so that he will not develop powerful habits of selfish indulgence. The rod is your divine enforcer. *"The rod and reproof give wisdom . . ."* (Prov. 29:15).

Please understand, we are not suggesting that a child can be trained into the Christian experience, only that his mind and body should be developed to their highest possible natural discipline. By elevating his standards and causing him to value truth and purity, you are aiding the Spirit in convicting him of sin, which, in time, will cause him to realize his need for a Savior. *This is the lawful use of the law* (1 Tim. 1:8).

CHAPTER 6

Guilt and Self-Loathing

CHILDREN NEED TO BE UNDER GOVERNMENT

Child training is not about causing children to function in a manner that is convenient for parents, nor are we interested in conditioning children to conform to community-established norms advantageous for society, which is the goal of progressive education. Rather, we want to empower children to ascend to the highest ideals found in human nature. To put it in modern speak: we train children to live according to their better angels. The Christian way of saying it is *we train children to walk after the Spirit and not after the flesh.*

So if we are going to cultivate children to live their humanity on the highest plane, we need to know something about human nature, for failing to take it into account would render our efforts futile by building on a false premise. The Bible is quite definitive in its doctrine of human nature, and, as would be expected, we find it in complete harmony with common observation.

Adam and Eve were created to live under the government of God. The original sin was Adam and Eve choosing to emancipate themselves from the authority of their Creator—to act independently and in defiance of the rule of law.

Upon disobeying, the couple experienced fear and shame, so they hid themselves from the presence of God (Gen. 3:10). Disobedience did not bring the satisfaction they expected—quite the contrary. They found themselves assailed by a judge within—the conscience. When guilty souls are faced with their faults, their first reaction is to blame someone else. Adam blamed

God for giving him the woman. Eve blamed the serpent. We see this pattern worked out in our children over and over again: They "didn't do it," or "didn't mean it," and if they did do it, it was "because he made me do it," so it is "not my fault."

GUILT

Most parents and many professionals fail to take into account the fact that all children experience guilt, and as parents it is our job to address the issue.

The human spirit given by God comes equipped with a resident, divine judge: the conscience. The conscience is nothing more than the mind knowing itself and passing judgment.

Every people-group entertains the same views on good and evil. There is found in the soul of every person a desire to be good coupled with guilt for being evil. The presence of religion in every culture is testimony to the universal sense of moral failure and the need to right what is wrong in the human soul.

The smallest child who knows he has failed in doing what he ought suffers guilt. At first his guilt is nothing more than personal disappointment that he has displeased those in his social circle, but as his soul matures he develops a sense of justice, fairness, honesty, benevolence, etc. and begins to value actions and people according to their conformity to these innate principles. When people in his life fail to be righteous, he blames them. Likewise when he fails to be righteous he blames himself. When one small child says to another, "You ought not do that," he is referencing a standard that exists in the soul of every human.

Guilt only occurs when one honestly judges himself to be worthy of blame. One may inappropriately be convinced of blame, but guilt is nonetheless self-incrimination for perceived wrongdoing. In some families much of the guilt children experience is not derived from moral failure; it is a product of not being loved and cherished by parents and friends and is better described as self-loathing. All guilt, if left unattended, will produce self-loathing. Child development specialists see the self-loathing and try to address that issue, but they do not have the tools to address guilt, the underlying cause.

SELF-LOATHING

To hold moral values is to judge. A person without judgment is a person without preference—that is, a non-person. As we judge others we judge ourselves. All judgments are accompanied with sensibilities (feelings). To fail to live up to one's own standards results in self-condemnation and guilt—bad feelings about self. Guilt is unavoidable self-accusation. It is the soul knowing itself and not liking what it sees.

A small child's soulish faculties are not completely operative; nonetheless, a child who violates his budding conscience becomes burdened with guilt and, if left unattended, self-loathing.

LOVING ONE'S SELF

In the extraordinary ignorance of modern child development "experts," many entertain the assumption that a child's major problem is "not loving himself." Their misdiagnosis comes from a failure to understand the association of the emotion of self-loathing with the supreme motivation of self-love. No one needs to be encouraged to love himself. Self-interest is an indispensable part of our human nature. We think in terms of what will benefit us. *"For no man ever yet hated his own flesh; but nourisheth and cherisheth it"* (Eph. 5:29). It is necessary to our survival and creativity to love ourselves, but self-love is a given, an unavoidable reality.

The higher one values self (loves himself), the greater his self-criticism when he fails to achieve his goals of "being good." The subsequent self-loathing is nothing but self-rebuke for failure to benefit the person he loves the most—HIMSELF. When a child is self-loathing, his conscience is condemning the self for not living up to the ideals of self-love. **Self-loathing is disappointed self-love. The more he loves himself, the deeper the self-loathing.** If he truly hated himself, he would find great satisfaction in his own failures.

This is not to discount the sad reality that some children become self-loathing because they are denigrated and abused, but their poor feelings about self are nonetheless rooted in self-love.

POSITIVE AFFIRMATION

Taking their cue from secular "wisdom," misguided parents try to build up their child's self-image by means of "positive affirmation." It is troubling to see parents trying to purge their children of guilt or low self-esteem with empty, sweet words. No child can be led from the pit of self-condemnation by heaping empty praise on him. He knows better. Unless the praise is earned, the child feels all the worse for the unfounded commendation. Praise and positive affirmation are indispensable nourishment to a child's soul, but the child must believe the praise is rooted in sincere reality.

GUILT AS A WEAPON

Bad behavior causes guilt, but so does rejection and ridicule if the child becomes convinced that he is the one in the wrong. Misguided parents sometimes use guilt to manipulate their children, or they shame and humiliate them in hopes they will be provoked to act in ways that will avoid the negative labeling. They may see the child temporarily acquiesce, but obedience performed out of the desperation of guilt only deepens guilt, putting the child further out of touch with true repentance and healing.

GUILT IS NEVER RESTORATIVE

Guilt is never in itself restorative. That is, it does not tend toward less blameworthy actions, for, though it directs the soul away from the activity causing the guilt, there is no strength or moral courage in guilt itself. On the contrary, the guilt-ridden soul is a slave to every temptation. Compounded guilt puts one out of touch with normal psychological restraints. The despair of accumulated guilt drains motivation to do right. The anguish of failure and the dreaded anticipation of it lowers one's expectations of self. Unresolved guilt lowers self-esteem to the point where one does not expect to do other than fail.

This reality has caused psychologists to view guilt itself as the culprit. To address guilt as if it were the disease is like dealing with the pain of a toothache but not the tooth. It feels good for the moment, but does nothing to cure the underlying cause.

Guilt is an essential part of our natural, moral self. Without it we would be like a smoke detector with no alarm. But guilt is only a means to an end, a temporary condition. It's the soul's equivalent of pain—when we touch something hot, it is designed to give us warning and a strong signal to change our actions. It is a great blessing to feel genuine guilt, both as a sign of life and as a healthy response to danger.

SELF-ABUSE

Guilty souls who are resigned to their condition are often seen inflicting pain and suffering on themselves. It is estimated that up to 15% of adolescents deliberately cause pain or wounds to their person. Some children are covered with scars from self-cutting; others have broken their bones. In some way, they are satisfying a need to suffer for their sins. This self-abuse is an unconscious attempt to "pay the fiddler." The conscience is indelibly imprinted with a conviction that sin deserves punishment. We intuitively know that wrongdoing not only deserves but will one day face punishment. From the earliest awakenings of conscience, a child is in the grip of this reality. It remains a basic presupposition of life.

The presence of guilt is the law's chief witness against the sinner. If guilt is not resolved, it will shackle the damned in the eternal misery of their sins. Like a zealous and fanatical prosecuting attorney, the conscience will not drop its case until it is sure that justice has been done. A guilty soul is a soul that feels it deserves punishment equal to the offense. This is an inescapable psychological reality. The guilt-burdened soul cries out for the lashes and nails of justice. That is why the soul of man never rests until the conscience has been purged by believing that Jesus suffered our condemnation in his own body.

RELEASE FROM GUILT

Understanding the role that guilt plays in a child helps us understand our role in training. If we allow self-indulgence and unruliness to thrive in the child, it will produce emotional instability. An undisciplined child will be insecure. Lack of self-control issues forth anger. A failure to get one's way causes self-pity. Unfulfilled lust generates restless agitation. Feelings of being treated unfairly incubate bitterness. We cannot prevent the ugly fruit that develops in an unruly child, but we can nurture him to act in ways that will make him feel good about who he is, and we can affirm his worth with our fellowship and words of praise. A well-balanced child or adult should be able to stand up tall and say with confidence, "Wow, it feels good to be me."

But there is a deeper aspect of guilt that cannot be purged with fair words and fruitful deeds. When a child knows he has acted unworthily, that he has been a bad person, hurting someone else with hands or words, or has been mean or cruel or ugly in any way, the guilt may be quieted with good deeds but it will not be purged. It builds up in the recesses of the soul to create a lifetime of disappointment before God and self. Most adults feel that the scale of justice is weighted against them and that if they got their due, they would suffer greatly. When tragedies happen to them, their first response is, "I am being punished for my sins."

> *If we confess our sins, he is faithful and just to forgive us our sins, and to cleanse us from all unrighteousness.* (1 John 1:9)

> *For by one offering he hath perfected for ever them that are sanctified.* (Heb. 10:14)

> *For I will be merciful to their unrighteousness, and their sins and their iniquities will I remember no more.* (Heb. 8:12)

> *[F]or I will forgive their iniquity, and I will remember their sin no more.* (Jer. 31:34)

> *Come now, and let us reason together, saith the LORD: though your sins be as scarlet, they shall be as white as snow; though they be red like crimson, they shall be as wool.* (Isaiah 1:18)

> *How much more shall the blood of Christ, who through the eternal Spirit offered himself without spot to God, purge your conscience from dead works to serve the living God?* (Heb. 9:14)

Mature teens and adults can find release from their guilt through the Savior who suffered the curse of their sins, but little children cannot yet understand that the Creator has been lashed and nailed in their place. Yet, parents need not wait until their children are old enough to understand the vicarious death of Christ to purge their consciences of guilt. God has provided parents with the position and the tools to purge children of their guilt and prevent self-loathing from taking hold. We cannot prevent them from feeling guilty when they knowingly act in ways that are hurtful, but we can provide an atmosphere of forgiveness and redemption. Above all, children need to know they are loved and cherished, that they are the most important thing in our lives. If they are going to trust us as mediators of God's forgiveness, they need to be convinced that we are worthy representatives of the law of God and have authority to dispense punishments and rewards.

The progressive (liberal, leftist, humanist, secularist) will agree fully with our assessment that the child needs to feel secure and cherished, but the secularist's toolbox is empty beyond that. Their philosophy does not admit to a divine conscience and of one's duty to moral law, so they have no answer to guilt other than denying its validity. They would try to eliminate the guilt by fudging on the standards or by pumping up the guilt-laden child with false self-worth through "positive affirmation," empty praise that may dull the guilt feelings but will never purge their little souls of the feeling that they have acted as they should not and are therefore unworthy of respect and admiration. The empty praise that ignores the root of their guilt may only deepen their sense of unworthiness.

THE POWER OF "ABSOLUTION"

Assuming the child is enveloped in hands of love and goodwill, nurturing parents have the instrument of chastisement that can absolve the child of guilt feelings, cleanse his soul, instruct his spirit, strengthen his resolve, and give him a fresh start through a confidence that all indebtedness is paid in full. This is a precursor to understanding the gospel of Christ. *"The blueness of a wound cleanseth away evil: so do stripes the inward parts of the belly"* (Prov. 20:30). *"Inward parts of the belly"* is a description of the physical sensations associated with guilt. Stripes (*"scourgeth"* Heb. 12:6) are said to be to the soul what the healing blood flow is to a wound. **A child properly and timely spanked is healed in the soul and restored to wholeness of spirit.** According to the Scriptures, a child can be turned back from the road to hell through **proper** spankings. *"Withhold not correction from the child: for if thou beatest him with the rod, he shall not die. Thou shalt beat him with the rod, and shalt deliver his soul from hell"* (Prov. 23:13–14).

Father, as high priest of the family, through a judicious use of the rod, you can temporarily relieve your child of his guilt and feelings of condemnation. Guilt gives Satan a just calling card and a door of access to your child. In conjunction with teaching and tying strings of fellowship, **the properly administered spanking is restorative as nothing else can be.** This is a highly offensive principle to unbelievers. They cannot understand it because they have no personal frame of reference, and they will interpret it to mean something repulsive. However, a number of Christian psychologists and psychiatrists are fully supportive of this fact of human nature.

But the natural man receiveth not the things of the Spirit of God: for they are foolishness unto him: neither can he know them, because they are spiritually discerned. (1 Cor. 2:14)

You theologians should understand that we are not suggesting that a parent's chastisement in any way redeems the soul of the child. But purging the emotions of guilt is a wonderful tool that enables the matured child to understand the atonement of Christ.

COMFORTING ROD

Do you comfort your child with the rod? If you have not seen the rod as a comfort, you have missed its purpose. *"Thy rod and thy staff they comfort me"* (Psalm 23:4). *"I will chasten him with the rod . . ."* (2 Sam. 7:14). *"Then will I visit their transgression with the rod, and their iniquities with stripes"* (Psalm 89:32).

David, who experienced the rod of God's correction and was chastened for transgression, found comfort in the divine discipline. The rod was a comfort to him. It assured him of God's control, concern, love, and commitment. Children need to know that someone who loves and cares for them is in control.

"Chasten thy son while there is hope, and let not thy soul spare for his crying" (Prov. 19:18). **Proper use of the rod gives new hope to a rebellious child.** Parents are exhorted to not allow the child's crying to deter them from administering corporal chastisement. **Parents' emotions can stand in the way of cleansing the child's soul of negative feelings.**

An unchastened child is not only restless and irritable in his spirit, but he causes the whole house to be in turmoil. *"Correct thy son, and he shall give thee rest; yea, he shall give delight unto thy soul"* (Prov. 29:17). A properly chastened child will find rest in his spirit and will give rest to his parents, thus increasing the fellowship and goodwill of the family.

Understand, when I say "properly chastened" I am again affirming that physical chastisement is indispensable in early training, but it reaps positive results only when administered by a wise parent in a thoughtful, gracious manner with deliberation. In this context, it achieves a state of peace and contentment in the soul of the child. Good medicine works only when it fits the disease and is properly administered.

I once observed a small child who, upon being caught in a misdeed, turned her backside to her parents, pulled her diaper down, and gave herself three slaps on the bare bottom. The offering, though cute, was not accepted. The lawgiver must administer this kind of chastisement in order to effectively remove guilt. A child knows but one lawgiver—his parents.

Keep the standards high, as high as the person of Christ. Let the guilt come, and while the child is yet too young to understand, purge his guilt by applying the rod when you know he has willfully violated the rule of law. When he finally matures to the point of understanding, having experienced the process of cleansing many times, he will readily grasp the principles of atonement through the vicarious death of Jesus Christ.

If you or your spouse or any of your friends have reason to believe that the corporal chastisement you administer is not producing positive results in removing your child's guilt but may be harmful, do not keep spanking. Get some advice from parents who are achieving very positive results.

THERE WAS A MIRACLE HERE TONIGHT

Recently, a young couple with five children came to us for advice. The wife had become unresponsive to her husband and irritable with their three children under five. "I sometimes feel like I am going crazy. I don't want to have any more children," she blurted out.

Being personal friends of ours, they stayed in our home for a couple of days, submitting to scrutiny. After a little instruction about consistent training and the proper use of the rod, they went home and gave it a try. Two weeks later they were in a church meeting where I was speaking. Their children all sat on the bench with them, never making a stir. Afterward, the father, eyes filled with wonder, exclaimed, "There was a miracle here tonight, and no one seemed to notice." As I was looking around for discarded crutches, he continued, "A whole service and not a peep out of them! I can't believe it!" A little training and a little discipline with the rod, and the children gave their parents rest and delight. Furthermore, the children were obviously happier. The mother later said, "Now I think I would like to have more children."

THE MAGIC WAND

Don't think of the rod as a weapon of defense or as punishment; think of it as a "magic wand." The first time parents see its restorative powers, they are amazed. I still marvel at the power of the little rod when administered in love at the appropriate occasion.

Picture a child of any age: he is miserable, complaining, or perhaps defiant and a bully to other kids. When you look at him, all you see is the inside of a bottom lip. Every device has failed to bring relief. The kid acts as a partisan living in foreign, occupied territory. He is obviously plotting the day when he will throw off his yoke of bondage. Bribed, threatened, or swatted, he only gets worse. He is the perfect candidate for a dose of corporal chastisement. Fail to use the rod on this child, and you are creating a modern-day Nazi. After a short explanation about bad attitudes and the need to love, patiently and calmly apply the rod to his backside. Somehow, after five—or at the most ten—licks, the emotional poison is transformed into gushing love and contentment. The world becomes a beautiful place. A brand-new child emerges. It makes an adult stare at the rod in wonder, trying to see what magic is contained therein. *God would not have commanded parents to use the rod if it did not work something good in the child!*

TIME OUT ON TIME-OUTS

I know one young boy who is not spanked when he throws a tantrum or disobeys, so he throws a lot of tantrums. It seems he delights in doing what he shouldn't. The more he rebels, the meaner and guiltier he gets. For punishment, he is pinched in a retaliatory fashion or made to sit in the corner, or sometimes put in a dark closet. "Time-outs" tend to produce feelings of rejection. He is bad, so he is not wanted. When this obstinate kid comes out of isolation, he is madder than ever. He could intimidate a fire-breathing dragon.

His parents bought in to the "time-out" fad before he was born. It seems he needs time-outs more often and for longer periods, yet they serve no purpose but to give the parents a break. Sitting in a corner, he was heard to say, "Nobody likes me. I'm as bad as the Devil. I never do anything right." This little fellow is being reared to take his place in a jail cell. Dark corners and dark closets breed darkness in the soul. An empty room and a pouting child incubate guilt and anger. Only the rod and reproof bring correction. Somehow children know the rod is their just due. The rod is a gift from God;

use it as the hand of God to train your children. When administered by parents who also tie strings of fellowship, it is the compassionate approach to child training.

Dr. Justin Coulson, who doesn't believe in "smacking kids," also doesn't believe in time-outs. In an article called "The Trouble with Time-Out," Coulson says, "Time-out is really a politically correct euphemism for something I'm more inclined to call 'forcible isolation.'" He says it is a "withdrawal of love and attention." He says that a child subjected to time-out "is more likely to sit and stew about her punishment—and if another sibling was involved she may also start plotting her revenge." He is totally correct on this one point. He thinks time-out leaves kids in greater emotional distress for longer periods than smacking! Coulson offers alternatives that are theoretically lovely, but in practice are useless. Time-outs provide fertile ground for the incubation of guilt and self-loathing in the heart of the child.

CHAPTER 7
What Would Rover Do?

ANIMALS EMPLOY CORPORAL DISCIPLINE

Studies of human behavior often reference nature for examples of normative human behavior. A discussion on the psychological benefits of breastfeeding for infants will note the practices of other mammals. Colts raised on a bottle, who never had a mother's care, are notoriously difficult to train and are prone to dangerous behavior toward both other horses and humans—kicking, biting, pushing, etc. Every farmer knows that a chick hatched in an incubator and raised without a hen is not likely to sit on her eggs and care for her young because she has never experienced parental nurturing. We see the same behavioral pattern in children raised in an orphanage from birth; without having experienced loving parental care, when they are grown they tend to be deficient in parenting instincts. Any animal not socialized when young will lack confidence when older and will have aggressive tendencies, just as does a child who experiences limited human contact as an infant. As animals must be nurtured and trained, so must humans, and in much the same manner.

Some Christians will be offended (and a few leftists will pretend to be) by our comparing human parenting to animal behavior, but God commands, *"Go to the ant, thou sluggard; consider her ways, and be wise"* (Prov. 6:6). And again, *"But ask now the beasts, and they shall teach thee; and the fowls of the air, and they shall tell thee: Or speak to the earth, and it shall teach thee: and the fishes of the sea shall declare unto thee"* (Job 12:7–8). Wow! I bet you didn't see that one coming.

So it is a well-established practice and a biblical command to look to animal behavior to find models for human behavior, which begs the question at hand: Do animals employ corporal chastisement on their young? The answer is a resounding YES.

DOLPHINS

Bobbie Sandoz-Merrill, in her popular book *In the Presence of High Beings,* says of dolphins, "To establish discipline and boundaries with their young as well as with others, wild dolphins generally use posturing gestures such as tail-slapping, tooth-raking, or face-to-face head-nodding, which may culminate in jaw-clapping. When dolphins and whales can't get the surrender they need from their young, they may hold them underwater for longer than is comfortable in order to re-establish their dominance and parental authority." Tooth raking is the act of swimming by and raking the youngster with a tooth. It creates a little pain without actually doing damage. It is not punishment, in that it is not punitive, but it certainly is corporal chastisement designed to teach the young to avoid certain behaviors.

The newsletter of the Wild Dolphin Foundation says, "If the youngsters get too out of line, the adults will discipline them by snapping their jaws, pushing them with their rostrums, slapping them with their tails, biting, or holding them at the bottom." Dolphin mothers discipline their young by pushing them to the bottom and raking their noses on the sandy, shell-strewn ocean floor.

Dolphins have been observed disciplining a three- or four-day-old calf for wandering off too far. When the distressed mother locates her calf, she repeatedly tosses it into the air. This physical display is no doubt unpleasant to the calf and is a warning that it is dangerous to stray too far from Mother.

The intelligence of animals is amazing. Somehow the mother knows that the future survival of her young depends upon her communicating the need to exercise caution and discipline. She never punishes them (a lesson to overwrought parents), but she very deliberately trains them to exercise self-control.

The many examples of nature teach us that the true purpose of discipline is not to wound the young, but to instruct them. All true and effective discipline is done in the context of teaching, whether of animal or child.

One observer recounts a personal experience, "Dolphins seem to use the crisscross behavior to check out boats. When [one mother] saw her calf crisscross our bow, she shot through the water to her calf. Next thing you know, the calf shot out of the water to avoid its mother. The calf cleared its mother's irritated lunge and, peace restored, they swam off together into the sunset."

It is common to observe horses, cats, and dogs as they reprimand their young with a quick nip. Chimps and gorillas will nip and/or swat with their hands.

KOALA MOTHER SPANKS HER YOUNG

Ambrose Pratt, in *The Call of the Koala* (Robertson & Mullens, 1937), recounts a scene typical of the koala community. A mother koala, Angelica, is attempting to train her baby, Edward, to climb safely. When he acts in ways she considers dangerous, she spanks him soundly.

> He ascended a few feet quite cleverly, but all of a sudden his heart failed him, and there he stuck fast like a limpet, unable to advance or recede, and squalling with terror. Angelical went to his assistance, took him in her arms, returned to her place and gave Edward a mild spanking, repeatedly addressing the palm of her hand to the spot where bears (and most other animals) sit down. I doubt if there is anything more ludicrous to be seen on this earth than the spectacle of a mother koala chastising her child. She does it precisely in the same way as a human mother, and in the doing of it she wore that expression (so awfully familiar to erring juveniles the wise world over) which says more plainly than words: 'This hurts me more than you, my son. I do it only for your good!'
>
> Edward got many a spanking in the weeks that followed, for every day he grew more venturesome and less afraid of falling into the terrible unknown void beneath his lofty perch. In addition he became very mischievous, and he gave Angelica several nasty frights by climbing along very thin boughs, where she dared not follow him. Of this habit she finally cured him by administering a really sound thrashing. It was no use crying or whaling. Angelica was merciless. Some humans in a motorcar heard the outcry and stopped to see what was the matter. They entered the paddock and soon located the scene of the brawl. "Hi! Hi! Hi!" they shouted. Angelica blandly ignored them. They became indignant at her for beating the baby and tried to make her desist by loud shoo-ing and by throwing sticks

at her. Angelica eyed them with benevolent indifference and continued beating her baby. When she had given him all she believed he deserved, and not before, she let him go, and, with the air of one who had nobly performed an objectionable duty, and merited reward, she curled up and closed her eyes. The whimpering Edward scurried up a neighboring bough, sat down, and began to wail like a very unhappy dingo.

Angelica endured the noise for precisely one minute, then suddenly she uncurled herself and, with astonishing agility, she rushed upon the naughty one. Edward, preoccupied with his lamentable vocalizations, was taken by surprise. At the last second he tried to escape, but a long arm and strong paw detained him. This time Angelica did the job thoroughly, and she continued to spank the luckless Edward until he ceased squealing and adopted the role of a silent penitent. Angelica was immediately mollified, and she cuddled the sobbing little body to her breast. A moment later both were apparently sound asleep; and far down below a man's voice was heard to exclaim: "My sainted mother! What do you know about that?"

MAN'S BEST FRIEND

The animal we are most familiar with is the family dog. Many of us have read a book or at least several articles on dog training. Puppies bite when they play. The only way they know whether they're biting too hard is if someone tells them—and that someone is their mom. Mom might first withdraw and stare at them. If the bad behavior continues, she may then growl and show teeth. If the puppy still bites, she will bite back—not hard enough to puncture the skin, but enough to communicate that biting is an unpleasant experience.

If you take a puppy away from its mother too early, it will have a tendency to bite too hard when playing—even drawing blood. But if you leave it with Mom a few more weeks, it will have learned to be gentle because she employed corporal discipline to teach it to respect boundaries.

Naomi Millburn discusses on dailypuppy.com why mother dogs bite their puppies. "Mother dogs teach their puppies to respect authority." She is correctly assuming that the puppy *needs* to be subject to authority, whether it wants to or not. Millburn says, "Mother dogs sometimes use biting as a technique for general discipline . . . If a puppy is acting too aggressively with the rest of the litter, his mother might bite him on the muzzle to get him to cut it out." She asserts, "This type of training is especially crucial for young pups who display especially dominant, assertive, and forceful temperaments."

Canine Mom also uses physical discipline to maintain order in her family. If a puppy crowds out its siblings or gets aggressive with them, she will nip it on the muzzle as a sign to cease its aggression. She's not aggressive, but she *is* assertive. If a nip doesn't do the job, then she will raise the level of discipline to the point where her puppy stops the unwanted behavior. She will win the contest of wills. In nature the mother always wins—for the sake of her offspring.

Now if the mother dog could read, she would be told by progressive, dog-behavior specialists (who never owned a dog) that when mama dogs bite their puppies, the tots will grow up to be biters. She would also be told that if she just loves her puppy and makes him feel good about who he is, then he will eventually grow out of it and be the better for it, not having been stymied by feelings of self-loathing caused by Mother's growls of rejection and "aggressive corporal punishment."

Mother dog is not punishing her pup, just as traditional Christian parents do not punish their children. Punishment and discipline are not the same thing. Punishment requires children to suffer for their mistakes, whereas discipline teaches children to learn from their mistakes. Proper physical chastisement is a teachable moment that produces positive results in every way. Discipline is where the teachable moments exist. It is where you can step in and teach self-control, cooperation, social skills, and obedience to the rule of law.

Nature also provides another insight. Once the young have felt the little pain of a nip from Mom, thereafter just a show of teeth and a growl are enough to elicit a positive response. She may never have to bite again—just threaten to. So it is that parents who have applied the rod to the backside of their children and demonstrate a readiness to do so again if needed will find that a growl (or *that look*) carries the same weight as a bite. Parents who are consistent in winning the contest of wills hardly ever have to actually spank their children.

So those of us who adhere to traditional parenting find indisputable support in nature for the judicious and measured use of corporal discipline.

CHAPTER 8

Attack on Traditional Child Training

WHAT "STUDIES" SHOW . . . AND WHAT THEY DON'T

In 1946, Dr. Benjamin Spock published his book *The Common Sense Book of Baby and Child Care.* At the time of his passing in 1998, it had sold more than 50 million copies and was translated into 39 languages. According to *The New York Times, Baby and Child Care* was, throughout its first 52 years, the second-best-selling book next to the Bible. In 1989 Dr. Spock, concerned over "the sky-high and ever-rising figures for murders within the family, wife abuse, and child abuse in America," concluded that, "[Physical punishment] certainly plays a role in our acceptance of violence. If we are ever to turn toward a kindlier society and a safer world, a revulsion against the physical punishment of children would be a good place to start." In the 1998 edition of *Baby and Child Care,* he said, "The American tradition of spanking may be one reason there is much more violence in our country than in any other comparable nation."

Some will say that Dr. Spock became a household word, the go-to authority on child rearing. He is arguably the father of modern, progressive child rearing. He influenced an entire generation of academics, his views quoted in textbooks and periodicals. When Dr. Spock said, "The American tradition of spanking may be one reason there is much more violence in our country . . ." he was inviting a horde of academics to prove his supposition. And they emerged in force, quoting one another and asserting as fact their anecdotal experiences. But most parents in America, though they had heard the name Spock, knew nothing of his views and went on rearing their children in the traditional manner, as had their parents before them.

Twenty-two years ago when we wrote *To Train Up a Child,* the growing movement among leftists to denigrate corporal chastisement, which they called "corporal punishment," had little influence on the parents of America. Most were unaware of the academic and professional assault on traditional parenting. Two decades have seen a significant shift. The universities and professional journals along with a complicit media have flooded parents with the undocumented assertion that "studies confirm that hitting children causes them to grow up to be violent, maladjusted, and emotionally ill," all the negative traits we see multiplying in public-school kids today.

If they were using the word *hitting* in its normal connotation, we could well agree with them, but when they say *hitting* they mean any and all forms of corporal discipline down to a mother slapping the hand of her child. Opponents make no distinction between measured, compassionate spanking and tyrannical, whaling, fist-pounding psychos.

In the quest for hearts and minds, the crusaders have seized the language: we say *spank,* they say *hit.* We say *paddle,* they say *beat.* We say *discipline,* they say *punish.* They choose inflammatory language designed to project violence onto classical parenting and shut down any who would speak up in its defense. They cause parents to hide their time-honored parenting as if it is something to be ashamed of. In the end, our silence will surrender long-established biblical parenting to the whining voices of left-leaning ideologues. In our age, it is understandable that parents hide in their holes like gophers under the telescopic sights of varmint hunters ready to trigger the metal-jacketed round to the head of any who would dare pop up. The lethal corporal-chastisement hunters now dominate the field, and they have seen to it that their voices alone are being heard.

It seems all that is needed is a title before one's name and a firm assertion that "studies confirm" for one to be believed. The "studies" are usually not named, and the public dare not question the opinion of a professional. So the trend in the United States for the past several decades has been to abandon corporal discipline in favor of increased use of alternate discipline methods—e.g., consequences, time-outs, or withdrawal of privileges.

As the agents of permissive parenting see the tide of public opinion turning in their favor, they have gone into a feeding frenzy, devouring tradition and common sense, and they are pooping out drugged children who are cutting themselves, killing one another, and committing suicide. As discipline collapses, the schools have become battlegrounds with over 10% of teachers suffering physical assault in their classrooms each year, and many more being threatened with physical harm. That is almost half a MILLION teachers assaulted or threatened by students who do not believe they are constrained by boundaries (statistics from a 2010 Department of Education report on violence in schools). And amazingly, after creating the problem, the professionals now point to the results as evidence that they need to further strip parents of the tools that once produced generations of responsible young adults who by and large acted responsibly and exercised self-control.

According to *HealthDay News* "Seven percent of American schoolchildren are taking at least one medication for emotional or behavioral difficulties." That is, over 3.5 million children are being drugged into acceptable behavior because today's parents and schoolteachers have given up hope of instilling discipline. How could they without the tools?

When I was in school in the '50s and early '60s, all students quietly complied without the use of drugs. Drugging a child was unheard of. Every teacher had a "board of education"—a wooden paddle—lying prominently on the desk, and the principal patrolled the halls with a two-foot-long oak paddle. I was on the receiving end only twice during my 12-year durance, and it kept me fully compliant. They were serious about the rules, so I was as well. Today teachers have no more power over their students than do street signs. John Dewey and Dr. Spock never imagined where their progressive philosophies would lead. I am sure they thought their ideas would produce a better world. They were sadly wrong.

Though at least 80% of parents admit to using some form of corporal chastisement on their children, most parents have been so influenced by the anti-spanking propaganda that the majority have ceased preemptive and consistent use of physical discipline and only do so when provoked by their anger, which is far worse than not spanking at all. For when parents spank out of a well-thought-out philosophy, they don't reach a dangerous level of frustration and explode into physical discipline as do parents who are trying not to spank. So the campaign has taken a larger toll than the 80% number suggests. If the families of America are a study group, sixty years have proven that as parents depart from traditional parenting and schools give way to free expression and non-coercive discipline, we reap an increasingly ugly harvest in America's youth.

Even with their failed experiment, the political move to outlaw spanking is gaining momentum. There will come a time in the United States of America when it will be a crime to use any physical discipline on your children. It is not a question of *if* but of *when*. A recent writer asked, "What spanking debate? There is only one side. Where are the advocates for spanking? There are none, nor can there be in the face of overwhelming evidence." They are overwhelmed with their own egos and their progressive agenda emanating from a leftist ideology: mother earth, abortion on demand, sexual license, evolution, global warming, re-distribution of wealth, suppression of the Christian religion, and Big Brother who takes over the responsibility of raising all children. The studies done with real scientific controls do not confirm the anti-spanking agenda; quite the opposite, as we will see.

ANTI-SPANKING STUDIES

Naysayers are wrong in their assertion that "all studies confirm . . . ." When they do reference a study it is taken from a select group of troubled, violent, or emotionally disturbed youth who have ended up incarcerated or as part of a treatment program. Since most children are spanked, the majority of troubled youth will have been spanked, and since they are troubled youth a disproportionally large number of them will have been physically abused—hit, beaten, or punished severely. We would be in full agreement with the professionals that the children who were genuinely physically abused are more likely to become delinquent or emotionally troubled. So with certainty, counselors will discover that a large number of antisocial youth were physically abused. But their studies fail to distinguish between measured spanking by nurturing parents and violent physical abuse. If they were to do a study of 1,000 Christian, homeschooled children who are spanked, they would grow weary searching for cases of abuse, and they would be shocked and—since it doesn't fit their philosophy—disappointed at the consistently beautiful fruit.

Ralph S. Welsh, PhD candidate and lecturer in the Department of Public Health Sciences at Clemson University, offers the perfect example of the methodology employed to support the anti-spanking agenda in his article "Delinquency, Corporal Punishment, and the Schools" ([1978] *Crime & Delinquency* 24 [3]: 336–354). Take note of the composition of his "study group":

"Early in my clinical career, I was alarmed to discover the inordinate number of <u>juvenile delinquents</u> who had been exposed to harsh parental treatment during their developmental years. I took the time to question my <u>delinquent patients</u> and their parents carefully and to tabulate the information regarding parental punishment practices." In the same article he says, "One extensive study helped to convince me that corporal punishment could not easily be viewed as a harmless American tradition, to be tolerated and supported. This study involved <u>seventy-seven consecutive juvenile court referrals,</u> fifty-eight boys and nineteen girls."

You will notice that the "studies" are taken from juvenile delinquents and juvenile court referrals. Symptom-based sampling, where you start with a selected group associated with given behavioral problems and work backward to determine a cause, is totally non-scientific. They know better, but they are desperate to "prove" a causative link to something they are philosophically opposed to.

Jason M. Fuller of the University of Akron Law School says in his article "Corporal Punishment and Child Development" ([2010] *Akron Law Review* 44 [1]), "[P]rofessional methodologists have found that anti-spanking studies are often structured to support the researcher's personal philosophy, instead of being structured to fairly analyze the results of physical discipline."

I can understand the frustration of counselors who must deal with broken children every day. Anyone would be desperate to place blame, but the leftist predisposition and the misdirected influence of their academic training leave them with tunnel vision. Their conclusions are not scientifically justified. Their opinions are emotionally driven. Understandable as it is, it is nonetheless inexcusable for the damage it does to children who will not receive traditional training in self-control, accountability, and responsible action.

SURVEY IN A STATE PRISON

In a state prison chapel with 36 prisoners in attendance, I conducted an informal survey. I asked, "How many of you experienced some sort of physical discipline as children?" All but one responded in the affirmative. At this point, one who was so inclined could say that the survey proves that "hitting children" will result in criminal activity—35 out of 36 were spanked.

But I went on to ask how many felt their spankings were justly administered. Twenty-eight felt the spankings they received were just and appropriately administered. Six said they were "beaten" as well. But thirteen said they were not spanked enough. When I asked how many felt that the "spankings or beatings" they received played some part in their crimes, none raised a hand. Since more than 80% of parents spank, one can expect that 80% of all juvenile offenders will have been spanked. However, correlation is not causation or even association.

SCIENTIFIC STUDIES

Marjorie Gunnoe, a developmental psychologist at Calvin College in Grand Rapids, Michigan, who is **not** a spanking advocate but is an open-minded researcher, questioned 2,600 people about being smacked. One-quarter of them had never been physically disciplined. The participants' answers were compared with such behaviors as academic success, optimism about the future, antisocial behavior, violence, and bouts of depression. According to the research, children spanked up to the age of 6 were **likely as teenagers to perform better at school and were more likely to carry out volunteer work and to want to go to college than their peers who had never been physically disciplined.** "The claims made for not spanking children fail to hold up. They are not consistent with the data," said Gunnoe. "I think of spanking as a dangerous tool, but there are times when there is a job big enough for a dangerous tool. You just don't use it for all your jobs."

Child psychologist Elizabeth Owens, scientist at the Institute of Human Development at the University of California, Berkeley, conducted a study. She concluded, "If you look at the causally relevant evidence, it's not scientifically defensible to say that spanking is always a horrible thing. I don't think mild, occasional spankings in an otherwise supportive, loving family will do any long-term harm."

Akron Law Review published a study that examined criminal records and found that children raised where a legal ban on parental corporal punishment is in effect are much more likely to be involved in crime.

Psychologist Aric Sigman states, "The idea that smacking and violence are on a continuum is a bizarre and fetished view of what punishment is for most parents. If it's done judiciously by a parent who is normally affectionate and sensitive to their child, our society should not be up in arms about that. Parents should be taught to distinguish this from a punch in the face."

Jason Fuller says that Sweden is ". . . an ideal laboratory to study spanking bans," for a generation ago it became the first nation to impose a complete ban on physical discipline. According to Fuller, police reports indicate that since the spanking ban, child-abuse rates in Sweden have exploded over 500 percent. Even just one year after the ban took effect, and after a massive government-run public education campaign, Fuller found that "not only were Swedish parents resorting to pushing, grabbing, and shoving more than U.S. parents, but they were also beating their children twice as often." After a decade of the ban, "rates of physical child abuse in Sweden had risen to three times the U.S. rate," and "from 1979 to 1994, Swedish children under seven endured an almost six-fold increase in physical abuse," Fuller's analysis revealed. More than half of Swedish schoolchildren are undergoing some sort of therapy in an effort to solve learning problems.

Kenneth Dodge, a professor at Duke University, conducted a long-term study of corporal punishment's effect on 453 kids, both black and white, tracking them from kindergarten through eleventh grade. Now that is a scientific study. When Dodge's team presented its findings at a conference, the data did not make people happy. They found that the more a child was spanked, the less aggressive the child was over time. The spanked black kid was overall less likely to be in trouble. Scholars publicly castigated Dodge's team, but Dodge—who remains adamantly against the use of physical discipline—was so horrified by such questions that he enlisted a team of fourteen scholars to study the use of corporal punishment around the world. The researchers failed to find evidence that spanking had negative effects.

Dr. Diana Baumrind of the University of California, Berkeley, aided by teams of professional researchers, conducted what many consider to be the most extensive and methodologically thorough child development study ever done. They examined 164 families for over a decade, tracking their children from age four to fourteen. Baumrind found that "spanking can be helpful in certain contexts" and discovered "no evidence for unique detrimental effects of normative physical punishment." The study also revealed that children who were **never** spanked tended to have behavioral problems, and were **not** more competent than their peers as other professionals had suggested.

If we were to adopt the methods of the professionals, reasoning backward from a select group, we could reference "studies" proving our point. For example, *USA Today* interviewed 29 CEOs of very successful businesses regarding the cause of their success, and in the process discovered that all 29 were spanked as children. Following their methodology we could conclude that spanking will lead to becoming a very successful CEO. Of course that was not a scientific study, and the correlation proves nothing except that spanking does not prevent one from becoming a successful CEO.

So actual scientific studies lend weight to what the Bible says: *"The rod and reproof give wisdom: but a child left to himself bringeth his mother to shame"* (Prov. 29:15).

All presidents of the United States, including Obama, were spanked as children, as were nearly all senators, congressmen, and military commanders. In a 2011 *USA Weekend* interview, First Lady Michelle Obama admitted to spanking her daughter Malia once or twice when she was little. Laura Bush told Dr. Phil she did the same to her twin daughters, Barbara and Jenna, when they were young.

In a three-way discussion on Fox News, host Arthur Aidala says he was "spanked with a belt" and thinks it was a "good idea." Gretchen Carlson said she "was spanked, but things have changed." Aidala and Jonna Spilbor, both prosecutors and defense attorneys, said they spank their children as well.

NEW YORK "STUDY"

On a flight to New York City to appear on TV, the woman I sat next to on the plane said she had spanked her children. The taxi driver said he had "walloped" the kids when it was needed, and they were all in college now or successful in business. The director of the show said she was spanked and spanked her kids as needed. The make-up ladies and the back-stage hands were all sympathetic with my position. Only the host of the show and his selected audience thought "all studies confirm that hitting children will cause them to be violent . . . ." He had no children, thank God. His husband could not conceive, for obvious reasons. And his star witness, a child psychologist, said that parents "cannot be trusted to exercise corporal punishment" because they are so angry and out of control, indicating that was the reason she could not trust herself to spank.

TO BE FAIR

If you draw a line through history at the point where spanking was abandoned, you will find that it coincides with significant increases in juvenile misbehavior, suicides, low self-esteem, self-loathing, and a general degeneration of society. You will also discover that where parents give up corporal chastisement, they resort to emotionally abusive methods such as screaming, insulting, and humiliating in order to control aberrant behavior.

We are not suggesting that the cessation of spanking is primarily responsible for the increase in juvenile misbehavior and crime. There are many factors, and this is not the place to discuss them. But just as we cannot say that lack of spanking causes delinquency, the progressive cannot say based on the "statistics" that spanking causes delinquency. However, in answer to the progressive claim that spanking is responsible for youth misbehavior, if the statistics do speak in regard to delinquency, they would say that the cessation of spanking has increased misbehavior in youth, not diminished it as they suggested would occur with its elimination.

YELLING, THE NEW SPANKING

Ralph Welsh of Clemson University said, ". . . some experts speculate that many families—apparently taking to heart research that indicates spanking can make kids more aggressive, angry, and lead to problems later in life—are instead turning to yelling as a way to control their children."

Amy McCready, founder of Positive Parenting Solutions, says, "Yelling is the new spanking. It's sort of the go-to strategy for parents . . . I think (this) definitely is a generation of yellers."

The Wall Street Journal (Sept. 4, 2013) published an article by Andrea Petersen with the attention-grabbing headline, "Study Says Yelling Is as Hurtful as Hitting." Petersen, referencing University of Pittsburg researchers, says, "Parents who yell at their adolescent children for misbehaving can cause some of the same problems as hitting them would, including increased risk of depression and aggressive behavior . . . ."

WHY SO MUCH HOSTILITY TOWARD CORPORAL CHASTISEMENT?

So what is it about traditional child training methods involving physical discipline that provokes such intense opposition? It would be naïve and simplistic to attribute an evil motive to those who want to forbid all corporal chastisement. They have reasons that, to them, are righteous.

Parents Cannot Be Trusted

From their perspective, parents cannot be trusted to exercise measured physical discipline. We believe those against corporal chastisement genuinely care for the welfare of children and are convinced that the only way to guarantee their safety is to forbid all physical discipline.

In one of my appearances on a national television show to advocate for a parent's right to employ corporal chastisement, there were several guests, specialists of one sort or another, all aligned against my position. The arguments of both the host and the guests were based on the assumption that parents could not be trusted to spank because in their anger they might harm the child. When I said, "But we never get angry because we know we have the tools to bring our children into happy compliance," a clinical psychologist specializing in child behavior blurted out, "But all parents get angry!" The Christian heart is a miracle they do not understand. The Christian culture and way of life where children are treasured and nurtured to become godly is an alien concept to the secularists who are preoccupied with their own success and pleasure.

Transferal

Those members of the media, professionals, and academics who interpret corporal chastisement as an act of violence come to the discussion with a set of assumptions rising out of their own experience and transfer their feelings and impulses to others. Knowing no other way, they project their attitudes and lack of self-control onto anyone who advocates for spanking. They see us through a mirror, attributing to us their own personal faults. History will show that parents have not abandoned corporal discipline for the reason that it proved to be ineffective, but because many parents have become ashamed of the way they apply it.

Parents who do not believe in spanking lack the ultimate tool to bring their children into compliance, so things get out of control quickly. Children become incorrigible, and parents get frustrated and angry; they yell, threaten, and intimidate, but to no effect. In their helplessness they feel like striking out, hitting the child, and they know their feelings are wrong. At that point they can understand how some parents end up abusing their children. This mother and father are good people, loving parents, concerned, compassionate . . . but angry. It scares them. They have to go somewhere to cool off, or they send the child somewhere for a "time-out" so the child is out of reach of their anger.

I heard a child behavior specialist who is opposed to spanking explain why time-outs were better. She said, "Time-outs are not only for the child, they are for us parents; it gives us time to cool down and think of rational ways to approach the impasse." I am glad they take their time-outs, because apparently they need to. They have enough self-awareness to know that if they spanked they would be abusive in heart if not physically, so their conviction against spanking is strengthened. They have personal reason to believe that spanking is losing control and acting in violence toward children. They think that those of us who do spank are just like them, exploding on our children. They have fallen in a pit they dug with a progressive shovel.

They don't even believe us when we tell them that we on-the-job parents who maintain the option of spanking if necessary do not reach impasses, and we do not get angry. We don't need time to "cool down." Our children are happy and obedient because we have all the tools, the time, and the patience to train them. Our most frequently used tools are smiles and hugs, but the kids know that somewhere in the bottom of our toolbox, or maybe in a kitchen drawer, is a divine enforcer that will be applied if necessary. The naysayers don't have a clue. I feel like a doctor with a polio vaccine in a third-world country ravished by the disease and the people refuse to be vaccinated because they are convinced it is harmful. Ignorance wrapped in ideology is profoundly invulnerable to reason. Ignorance with a degree and peer approval is a religion beyond the reach of common sense and scientific studies.

Out-of-Touch Parenting

The approval of corporal chastisement declines with the declining of parental involvement. Parents abdicate their role as mentors by sending their children off to school where good parenting is vacuumed up and replaced with pure secularism and hedonism. But the failure doesn't end when the kids return home after school. Parents find it convenient to turn their children over to be tutored by various forms of electronic media, shut off from the fellowship of family. These secular parents have never experienced the parent-child bond that enables them to hold the heart of their children and impart character. They are time-out parents with no time for the kids because they are always out.

When we allow children to raise themselves or be guided by a variety of vacillating caregivers, we become strangers and do in fact relinquish the right to impose our wills upon them and act with final authority. In time, time-out parents will hear their children say, "You have no right to tell me what to do." That never happens in the Christ-centered home.

Parents in today's secular settings are much more distant from their children than were parents in former generations. Children are more autonomous, and the emotional distance makes physical discipline seem invasive to both parent and child. I would be uncomfortable spanking my neighbor's kids, but I am probably closer to them than many parents are to their own flesh and blood.

You must earn the right to constrain a child to obedience, a constraint that may involve spanking. Truly, if a child resents the spanking as invasive, then it will be counterproductive. If you do not have the heart of the child, if the child does not feel the justice of the spanking and accept it as part of a program of love and goodwill to make him/her a better person, then it will not be productive. Absent, out-of-touch parents who leave a child to raise himself have no right to use a power play when it is self-serving or when provoked by anger to do so.

So it is quite understandable that modern, disassociated parents will be uncomfortable spanking their children, but they think the rest of us are as out of touch with our children as they are with theirs.

Stereotypes in the Media

Most people get their worldview from media. After a dozen movies featuring a Bible-thumping fanatic who tries to beat the fear of God into his wayward offspring while quoting Scripture and rebuking the Devil, even professionals come to believe the stereotype and attribute the same temperament to all traditional parents who practice corporal chastisement.

Years ago, when we first started homeschooling, even before the word *homeschool* was known (1976), we received several visits from child protective services (1982–83) and soon found ourselves before a judge in his private chambers. Without questioning us, the judge immediately launched into a diatribe referencing a movie he had recently viewed. He said, "I know your kind. I saw a movie the other night that had a bearded, Bible-thumping, tyrant of a father who kept his kids from the public eye, not allowing them to go to school, beating the fear of God into them, while he molested his daughters . . ." I was shocked! Isn't a judge supposed to be professional, above petty stereotypes? Angered, I interrupted, "Judge, the reason we don't have a TV in our home is because we don't want to be exposed to garbage like that. I don't know what kind of whip you've got to crack, but get to cracking it; I've got a hundred thousand dollars to see you in court." And I grabbed my wife by the hand and left straightaway. Many families rallied around us, as did the media. Fortunately, I was a personal friend of a state senator who made a few phone calls on my behalf. Within three years homeschooling was declared legal in Tennessee.

The media are walking around with a prewritten script of how spanking harms children, and they are looking for any news event that can be made to fit their narrative. They especially love it when abuse takes place in a "Christian" home. Each year in the United States there are around 1800 children abused to death by their parents. About once a year (1 out of 1800) the abuse takes place at the hands of "Christian" parents. While the other 1799 stories are ignored, the one involving Christians or homeschoolers becomes the story of the year. It will get all of the attention because it fits their agenda, promotes their anti-Christian, anti-traditional worldview. They try to make it look as if abuse is epidemic in the Christian community, a product of believing the Bible. You will hear members of the media and professionals dismissively quote the Bible, "Spare the rod and spoil the child." They are so unlearned, they do not even know that their hated quote is not found in the Scriptures.

Desperation

Professionals who work with children see more than their share of abused children, and it is true that a disproportionally small number of abusers are Bible-quoting, self-righteous, religious fanatics. After a while any compassionate person immersed in these sad affairs will become desperate to find the cause of abuse and institute policies that will make a difference— save children from being harmed by their parents. Many violent teen offenders do come from homes filled with violence where a parent, usually the father, withheld love and affirmation and used severe physical punishment on them as well as verbal abuse.

Homes with no hugs but plenty of hits—no compassion but lots of angry passion—will doubtless produce problem children. Some will act out in anger; others will withdraw into feelings of worthlessness. The counselor sees the belt and the fist and everything in him screams, "Stop it! Stop hitting children!"

When I appear on television or am interviewed by newspapers and magazines, I am frustrated by the lens through which the interviewers see me. They always have preconceived notions that are as foreign to reality as if they were accusing me of breeding space aliens in my greenhouse. They have this stereotype in mind and are looking for someone to pin it on. It is rudimentary prejudice. They strike down a straw man and never come near knowing anything about the real world of happy, healthy families. But in their tiny segment of the world, there are no happy families, no parents with self-control who employ corporal chastisement in a compassionate and measured manner for the benefit of the child. They know nothing of our cheerful world of love and goodwill. They, along with their spouses and children, are broken. If they could actually spend three days living in one of our homes, seeing us relate to our children, feeling the joy and freedom, they would weep for their loss. They look out from darkness and everything is dark. They do not have the "light of life."

Philosophically Driven

One's worldview, or philosophy of life, has more to do with what one believes on a variety of issues than it does logic and reason. That is why people of a given philosophy (i.e., conservative or liberal) cluster on certain issues. For example, you know that if a person is pro–gay marriage and anti–capital punishment, he will be pro-abortion and anti-spanking. Likewise, you know that if a person is pro–gun rights and wants to leave the Ten Commandments posted in the courthouse, he will support a parent's right to spank in moderation and he will support leaving "In God We Trust" stamped on our money. The first is known as a *liberal,* and the second is called a *conservative.* You could make two contrasting lists containing twenty issues and find that most of the population will accept one or the other list in its entirety. You will never see a balanced split.

Logically, a self-described compassionate person who is pro–gay marriage, anti–death penalty, and anti–gun rights, should be anti–baby killing as well, but the leftists' positions have nothing to do with logic or compassion. The conflicting positions are the product of a worldview that they are compelled to keep intact.

Progressives generally believe that all conservatives are racists and homophobes, love war, are willing to destroy the environment for one more dollar, want to make Christianity mandatory, burn books we don't approve of, and put people in jail for committing immorality. They also believe we are willing to beat the fear of God into our children so they will grow up to be self-righteous like we are.

There is an extraordinary arrogance running through liberal minds. They think Christian parents who still practice corporal discipline are "unenlightened," bound by primitive traditions rooted in superstition. In their worldview, mankind is ever evolving away from primitive man to a more enlightened and compassionate people. They believe that as mankind abandoned human sacrifice, we will also put away physical punishment of children. They think it is just a matter of cultural illumination.

The leftists are in the process of winning a crusade against reason and truth. They don't look at the facts; they arrogantly assume that "all studies confirm . . ." For them to be convinced otherwise on this one point would require a complete reversal of their entire worldview on a number of issues. If one position fell to logic, the entire ideology would crumble.

SECULAR VERSUS BIBLICAL WORLDVIEW

The differences are rooted in their contrasting presuppositions about *human origin, human nature,* and *divine accountability.* What one believes about these three will determine one's position on all major issues. The conservative (traditional) worldview of both Judaism and Christianity is that every soul is created by God, is of extreme value, and will exist forever in a state of good or ill as determined by God on Judgment Day. The liberal (progressive, humanist, secularist) believes that man is the product of random chance; he comes from nothing for no reason and will again become nothing with no consequences. The only truth is "my truth" and the only purpose is "pleasure where you find it."

The conservative does not believe in randomness or pointlessness in either nature or the human soul; all is created by God and is overseen by Him toward a glorious end. Love of God and neighbor with joy and peace are to be pursued. Selfishness, hate, greed, pride, and bitterness are to be eschewed.

Just as we acknowledge the physical laws governing our existence, we acknowledge the spiritual laws as well, knowing that all actions have consequences. Just as we are subject to the fixed laws of nature, we are subject to the fixed laws of the soul. Laws that are fixed, physical or spiritual, require—yea, demand—to be observed.

Liberal humanists, thinking we are the product of mindless chance, do not believe there is a divine creator and overseer of the laws of the universe; as such, self is the highest authority to which one must answer. To the liberal secularists, not believing in life after death, there is no accountability. Everything that gives pleasure is acceptable, with no judgment. The Judeo-Christian philosophy, on the other hand, believes *"God shall bring every work into judgment, with every secret thing, whether it be good, or whether it be evil"* (Ecc. 12:14). One word describes the liberal philosophy—*permissive.* One word describes the Christian philosophy—*accountable.* Therein lies the difference in child rearing principles: permissive parenting, or holding children accountable.

So what do these two opposing philosophies have to do with spanking? It is obvious that if a parent believes in a personal God and a day of accountability, and that the child is born with a propensity to selfish indulgence and lawless living and if left to himself he will degenerate into a most undesirable state of depravity, then that parent's approach to child rearing is going to be quite different from that of a parent who believes in nothing other than the licenses to indulge without consequences. The Christian parent will communicate personal responsibility to immutable law, instilling the habits of responsible action; whereas the progressive parent is reluctant to make judgments about right and wrong. The progressive parent promotes free expression, whereas the Christian promotes the concept of freeing oneself from the constraints of selfish flesh so as to be able to do as one ought rather than as one's passions dictate.

THE CRUX OF THE CHRISTIAN PHILOSOPHY

Christians and the Western world influenced by Judaism and Christianity believe in a kind of spiritual Newtonian law of moral action: for every human action there is a reaction that occurs in the divine sphere just as it does in the natural. Every moral (or immoral) action has matching consequences that push back in equal force. In short, we will reap what we sow. The reaping *may* come through natural law while we breathe the breath of life, but it will *certainly* come at the hands of the divine Lawgiver in a day of final judgment. Under natural law, drunks destroy their livers, and hate causes a multitude of diseases. In the hereafter, God will cast all drunks into the lake of fire (1 Cor. 6:9–10), and He will judge those who hate as if they had committed murder. There is no escaping accountability. Parents must prepare their children for the reaping process. Hate, greed, selfishness, and intemperance all have negative consequences in this life, but deadly consequences in the next.

> *And I saw the dead, small and great, stand before God; and the books were opened: and another book was opened, which*

is the book of life: and the dead were judged out of those things which were written in the books, according to their works (Rev. 20:12).

Seeing then that all these things shall be dissolved, what manner of persons ought ye to be in all holy conversation and godliness . . . (2 Peter 3:11).

God's law has teeth. His commandments are not suggestions, and the consequence for breaking them is not a time-out. When God says, *"Thou shalt not commit adultery,"* that is a commandment. When God says, *"Thou shalt not kill,"* including unborn babies, that is a commandment, not a suggestion. When God says all drunkards and liars will be cast into the lake of fire, we take that quite seriously. So when God gives us the responsibility to prepare precious little souls to live in a world that ends in eternity, and understanding the rules by which all is lost or won, we are committed to communicating reality to them. That reality of sowing and reaping begins in this life under natural law but terminates in eternity under divine law. When we say to our children, "Don't play in the street," that is a commandment. When we say, "Don't hit your brother," that is a commandment. When we say to a two-year-old, "Don't throw your food on the floor," that is a commandment. To gain compliance, we rely upon loving example, fellowship around a common lifestyle, patient rebuke, and encouragement; but if all else fails to turn the heart of our children, before we allow them to scoff at our commandments and treat them as suggestions that need not be obeyed, we will emulate the government of God and bring our children into judgment, relying upon the rod judiciously applied to their backsides, assuring them of the seriousness of law.

Spanking is not punishment. Its primary purpose is not to cause them to fear future violations. Rather, it is a definitive moment in rebuke that brings the full focus of the child to recognize the finality of our command, punctuating and reinforcing the rule of law.

Corporal chastisement wisely applied communicates to children both authority and responsibility. The entire program of nurturing, instructing, affirming in love, commanding, and holding accountable by various means, with the possibility of a spanking as the ultimate enforcer, emulates the world into which they will eventually emerge—a world where all choices have consequences. It is a logical outflow of the Christian worldview in that it enables the parent to place the child in a dispensation patterned after divine reality. For the sake of the child, parents emulate the government of God by placing the child under divine law and then enforcing that dispensation by requiring accountability for lack of conformity.

It Bears Repeating:

Christian parents use corporal chastisement as a small but vital part of a program to emulate the present and future world where all actions have permanent and irreversible consequences. Without discipline, lawlessness and depravity progress unhindered. Due to the fallen human condition, children require a dispensation of tight management under penalty of law. Children raised thus will not clutter the court dockets later on.

Lack of absolutes and unenforced boundaries engender permissiveness. Children must be raised in a context of accountability and consequences for them to respect the concept of law.

The natural condition of children renders them opposed to achieving a higher state of being. Discipline and self-denial are foreign to human nature and must be learned and practiced. If left to their own devices, children will develop the worst of traits early, in their first seven years.

THE CRUX OF THE ANTI-SPANKING PHILOSOPHY

For reasons that are not justified by history, the secularists (humanists, liberals, socialists, leftists) believe that mankind is basically good, and if no artificial standards (as they say are found in religion) are imposed upon children, they will grow up without guilt or emotional hang-ups. The liberal philosophy is: Just love children and don't do anything to hurt them, and they will grow up to be delightful adults. In contrast, the Christian philosophy is that if you don't do anything, children will grow up to be selfish sinners lacking self-control. The liberal chooses not to invade a child's soul with absolutes and moral mandates that may cause guilt, thinking if the conscience is just an animal instinct, you don't need to regard it.

The secularist loves his children and tries to instruct them, but in the showdown of wills, the child is allowed to win in hopes that with maturity he will choose a more productive path. A few kids do raise themselves and turn out to be solid citizens, but most contribute to the decline of civilization and the overall depravity of humanity.

A society without Christian parenting is a society with a soul that will disintegrate in corruption as *"every man does that which is right in his own eyes."*

This section on the anti-spanking philosophy is rather short compared to the Christian worldview, but when one doesn't believe anything, it is difficult to find many words to describe it.

PROPHETIC WORDS

In this post-commonsense era of child rearing, let the near-prophetic words of **B. A. Robinson** (religioustolerance.org) resound in the ears of the social planners:

> If corporal punishment advocates are correct, then the abandonment of spanking will significantly increase violence and criminal activity among the next generation of adults. Society will become more violent. More people will be victimized. We will have to build additional jails to hold all of the criminals.

> If corporal punishment opponents are correct, then the abandonment of spanking will greatly decrease youth rage and criminal activity among both teens and adults. Over the longer term, levels of clinical depression, clinical anxiety, alcohol and other drug addiction among adults will also decrease.

Jason Fuller, in his article "Corporal Punishment and Child Development," reveals some startling facts: "From the 1980s to the 1990s alone, juvenile arrests for violent offenses increased by over 50%, and the rate of homicide by youths increased by 168%. Now American teens murder about 2300 people every year."

We now have a history that can testify to the fruit of abandoning corporal chastisement in the homes and schools. Need we say more?

CHAPTER 9

Applying the Rod

EXCESSIVE DISCIPLINE

Disciplinary actions can easily become excessive and oppressive if you set aside the tool of training and depend on discipline alone. I observed a proud, stern father ruling his children with a firm hand and making sure everyone knew it. His rod was swift to fall, especially in the presence of company. His children trembled in his presence, fearing to incur his displeasure. I wondered why, if he was so firm and faithful to gain obedience, he had not achieved it before entering the public arena. I was impressed, but not in the way he hoped.

Except where the very smallest children are concerned, training at home almost entirely eliminates the need for public discipline. Yet, should the need arise in public, be discreet with your discipline, and then go home and re-train in that area of behavior so that you and the child will not be placed in that difficult situation again. Proper training eliminates the need to spank a child either publicly or privately.

TO DO MY DUTY

When exhortation and encouragement have failed, and the time comes that it will be profitable to apply the rod, take a deep breath, relax, and pray, "Lord, make this a blessing to my child. Cleanse him of ill temper and rebellion. May I properly represent you in this chastisement." Don't be hasty or raise your voice. The child should be able to anticipate the coming rod by your utterly calm and controlled spirit.

At this point, the untrained child may panic and rush to demonstrate obedience. That won't happen after a few days of training. Never reward *delayed obedience* by suspending the sentence. And unless all else fails, don't drag the child to the place of cleansing. Part of his training is to come submissively. However, if you are just beginning to institute training on an already-rebellious child and he runs from discipline, too emotional to listen, then you must constrain him. Don't be hasty or frightening, but if you have to constrain him to spank him, do not hesitate. Hold the resisting child in a subdued posture for several minutes, or until he is calm, all the while explaining to him in a quiet voice why you are forced to spank him. Demonstrate that you are not going to be deterred by his theatrics. Let your actions show that you are unmoved by his protests. You are to rule over him as a benevolent sovereign. Your word is final.

You won't have to go through this dramatic process of constraining him more than two or three times. Once the child recognizes there is no escape, he will accept the futility of resistance and surrender to the inevitable. If he remains terrified, you need to re-examine your demeanor and invest in more face time. If you terrify your child, then you are terrifying and should make some serious adjustments before you try to exercise forceful constraint upon a scared youngster.

When you administer corporal chastisement, tell the child to bend over on the bed or couch. While he is in this position, admonish him— you have his undivided attention. Slowly begin to spank on his upper legs and buttocks. If you are too hasty, you may not allow time enough for the inner transformation to occur. You don't want him to get worked up to an emotional pitch so as to lose focus as to why he is being spanked. Remember you are not punishing him or trying to instill such an impression that he is scared to repeat the actions lest he meet with this terrible end again. You are gaining his attention so you can admonish his soul.

Use your own judgment as to what is effective. I have found that two licks on the small child and five to ten licks on older children are sufficient. As the child gets older, the licks must become more forceful if the experience is going to be effective in gaining heart compliance. Remember, **a spanking is made effective not by its severity, but by its certainty.** Spankings don't have to be as hard when they are consistently applied. **Your calm dignity will set the stage to make it more effective.**

If you are just starting the process of training a child who is not convinced of your authority, one spanking may not be enough. A general rule is to continue the correction process until the child has surrendered his will to you. If after a spanking followed by exhortation he is still rebellious, and you feel that further spanking is in order, you will want to lighten up on the force you apply. You can win the contest of wills only when the child is emotionally stable enough to make a rational decision to surrender to the powers that be.

Spanking is only part of the disciplinary action—the attention-getting part. It is the admonition part and the fact that you always win the contest of wills that serves to train the child to obedience. Remember, a child who is emotionally charged is not thinking clearly. So slow down, exhort him, allow him to calm down, and give him space to contemplate the reason for this disciplinary marathon. If there is ever an occasion when you feel it is necessary to give him more than about ten swats, be sure to lighten up. If you are leaving marks on the child that last longer than ten minutes, you are spanking too hard.

One warning: If an older child senses that the one spanking him is just exploding emotionally, venting his own feelings, he will react to the spanking much as he would if he were being whipped by an older, bigger boy at the playground. He will become subdued and cautious, but not honoring. It may control his actions for the moment, but it will not improve his attitude.

INSTRUMENTS OF LOVE

Men, make it a point never to use your hand for spanking. Exceptions should occur with full knowledge of the dangers an adult hand can inflict upon a small child. Ladies with wimpy, feather-like hands may swat their children with no harm being done, but most men should not spank with their hands. Furthermore, where the child is concerned, hands are for loving, not martial arts. A hand on a diapered bottom is useless as a spanking, but it is effective in causing permanent damage to the spine. There is no surface pain to the child thus struck. Any pain would be deep inside, similar to a fall or a car wreck.

Rather than the hand or a heavy instrument, it is more effective to swat the child with a light instrument against bare skin where nerves are located at the surface. A surface sting will cause sufficient, light pain, with no injury or bruising.

There is another reason why an instrument is better than the hand for spanking; it prevents the impatient, personally offended parent whose hand continually darts out like a snake from striking the child out of frustration. The hand-swatting can become a release of the parent's irritation. That is not training, and it can be emotionally abusive.

Select your instrument according to the child's size. For the child less than one year old whom you are conditioning to obedience, a thump with the finger is effective, or a small, ten- to twelve-inch-long, willowy branch (stripped of any knots that might break the skin), about one-eighth inch in diameter is sufficient. Always keep in mind that the small child is too mentally undeveloped to benefit from chastisement. Swatting a small child on the back of the hand or on an exposed leg is effective in conditioning them to obedience, but one so young is never punished. One or two licks on the back of the hand is enough to condition behavior. For the larger child that is actually spanked, a light belt or a two-foot switch is effective. Most kitchens contain a good variety of instruments in the form of wooden spoons, rubber spatulas, etc.

If, after training them for a week or so, you discover that five or ten licks are not sufficient, you have other problems in the relationship that will need to be addressed. Talk to a like-minded friend who has happy, well-trained children.

A CAUTION TO RECIPIENTS OF THE MILLSTONE AWARD

There are always some who act in the extreme. These individuals are capable of using what has been said about the legitimate use of corporal chastisement to justify ongoing aggression toward their children. I can think of several right now. They don't think of themselves as abusive. They would boast that they are "strong disciplinarians." *"But whoso shall offend one of these little ones which believe in me, it were better for him that a millstone were hanged about his neck, and that he were drowned in the depth of the sea"* (Matt. 18:6).

FORMS OF ABUSE

Average parents are quite predictable in their "discipline." They go through a warm-up exercise of threats and increasing irritation until their anger generates a temperament to retaliate against the child. They "lose it" and what follows is an altercation, but not biblical chastisement. Only a few parents are categorically abusive, but many parents sometimes give in to anger and employ abusive methods when sufficiently provoked: The child is rebellious. Like a whirlwind, father snatches the child up by the arm and gives him several bangs on the bottom. The father's eyes burn, his brow hardens. His pulse rate soars. *Anger* is the best word to describe his feelings. Smash! Subdue! "You will do what I say. You are not going to do this to me, little boy!" Red-faced, muscles tensed. Anyone looking at the face of a parent in this state would think there was a war in progress.

A tired and frustrated mother screeches, "Johnny, stop climbing on that stool. You could break something. Did you hear what I said? I am not going to tell you again. What do you mean, 'No?' You do what I tell you to—right now. DO YOU HEAR ME?!! GEEETT DOWNNN!!! I have had about all I am going to take from you. Why are you always so hard-headed? You are driving me crazy! This is absolutely the last time I am going to tell you! GET DOWN!!!" Then she tells him several more times. She has set up a competition between her intimidating emotions and the couldn't-care-less kid. A cauldron of anger and resentment has built up in this mother who is momentarily at a near-killing rage. Her hostility gushes forth. Her arm becomes a bungee cord, yanking the child from the stool, swinging him screaming through the air. With the other bare hand she strikes out at his bottom in a wild spray of flat-handed karate chops. The gyrating child, his little shoulder nearly dislocated, screams his protest and defiance. The mother has vented her anger. Her feelings of personal injury are expelled through this act of violence (that's what it is in the case described) and she is, for the moment, placated. The child flees from sight, going off to plot his next caper. She is satisfied that "He will not cause ME any more trouble for a while." This has no more resemblance to discipline than does a playground fight. It is these exact feelings that lead to the death of five children every day in the U.S. at the hands of their parents.

Spanking and swatting should never be an outlet for parents' anger. In the daily course of life, many people experience anger and have an impulse to strike out. There is no place for this selfish, vindictive streak in the discipline of children. I am ashamed to say that **in most cases, spankings are administered at the end of an intolerance curve.**

A wise parent is going to patiently instruct the child for his own good. **The rod must be accompanied by reproof in order to give wisdom (Prov. 29:15).** By *reproof*, we don't mean ranting and raving. You reprove a child by explaining why his behavior is unacceptable and offer explanation on how he should conduct himself. The child should hear concern and compassion in the parent's voice, not condemnation and threat. One of the marks of the unbalanced use of the rod is the lack of accompanying instruction. *"The rod and <u>reproof</u> give wisdom"* (Prov. 29:15). Where there is just a venting of the parent's anger, there will be no careful, patient, concerned reproof. The rod should be viewed as an aid to instruction, in that it reinforces reproof. It should never be the last resort, forced on us by our frustration. Reproof without the rod is equally unbalanced, for it leaves the impression that the law has no teeth.

Anxious parents who know they lack self-control and the ability to be objective and fair in discipline fear themselves and are afraid to use the rod, riding the pendulum to the extreme. They think the problem is solved if they just refrain from spanking, but because they are unwilling to repent and bring their own life into balance, their children suffer from lack of proper administration of the rod.

Parents must earn the right to use physical chastisement on their children. The many long hours of having fun together, working together, and just being a vital part of their lives are an absolute prerequisite to corporal chastisement. **A parent who does not show up to read a book, tell a story, or look at the child's latest creation should not show up to administer a spanking.**

CHAPTER 10

Philosophy of the Rod

THE TEACHING ROD

For a little while, God has placed the soul of your child under your tutelage. I must remind you again, your home is a moral workshop where you help God prepare your child for heavenly citizenship. The developing child benefits from growing up in a home that mimics the government of God. Proper application of the rod is essential in causing the child to understand the judgment of God—and eventually the grace of God.

As you were created in the image of God, your parenting should be in the image of God's government. In the limited world of the child, parents are representatives of truth and justice, dispensers of punishment and reward. A child's parents are the window through which he develops a view of what God is like and how moral government functions. You are also preparing him to navigate within the laws of society, the work place, and the legal system. If you make rules and do not respect them enough to enforce them, you will be making a negative statement about law in general. Your responses to transgressions are stage-playing the responses of God and all other authorities all the way down the chain of command. By proper application of the rod, children will come to understand the concepts of law and accountability. Unless all transgression, rebellion, and meanness of spirit are treated as God treats sin, the child's worldview will be false. If temporal authorities do not honor the law enough to enforce it with punishment, why should the child expect the great, eternal Authority to be any different?

The military uses real bullets in training men to avoid enemy fire. Replacing the rod with hollow threats would be to your children like replacing live bullets with blanks. It would get the men killed later in real battle.

THE FEAR OF GOD

A child must take seriously the moral law. *"The fear of the LORD is the beginning of wisdom"* (Prov. 9:10). In defining the root of sin, Paul said, *"There is no fear of God before their eyes"* (Rom. 3:18). The proper use of the rod does not cause the child to be afraid of his parents, but it teaches a wholesome fear, as when we adults fear the police and the courts to the point of obeying the law. Do not fall victim to the modern rewriting of fear as respect. For Jesus said, *"But I will forewarn you whom ye shall fear: Fear him, which after he hath killed hath power to cast into hell; yea, I say unto you, Fear him"* (Luke 12:5). The Scripture makes a distinction between honor, love, and fear: *"Honour all men. Love the brotherhood. Fear God. Honour the king"* (1 Peter 2:17).

Though we don't have *"the spirit of fear,"* we who understand eternity *fear* to be in opposition to the Avenger of all evil. Remember, you are preparing your children for real life in a real world, where they will face the consequences of their actions. From the cops to the IRS to one's employer, the world must be navigated with a healthy fear. And in the end, there is a real God in a real judgment of real accountability to a real reward in a real eternity. This is no game; the rewards are great, the loss too horrible for a parent not to make this the top priority. Use of the rod is not optional with a Bible believer. It is part of God's design for proper training and conditioning of children who will live in today's world, and especially in the world to come. The eternal souls of your children are at stake.

UNDERSTANDING GRACE

The end a Christian has in view for his children is not simply submission to the rule of law; we want our children to understand the grace of God. Only through the naked "sword" of the law are we pressed into an understanding of grace. The law is *"our schoolmaster to bring us unto Christ"* (Gal. 3:24). God could not show Himself on Mount Calvary until He first showed Himself on Mount Sinai.

By strictly enforcing the rules of the household through legislation, accountability, and punishment, you not only teach your children to fear and respect the Lawgiver, but you create opportunities to demonstrate grace when they commit any punishable offence and later show repentance. You can then show grace by suspending the penalty. What a teachable moment!

CHAPTER 11

Selective Subjection

I DON'T HAVE TO OBEY YOU

Some children have a very irritating habit—selective subjection. Have you ever tried to correct a child, only to be impudently told, "You are not my mother. You can't tell me what to do"? (Most likely, the mother can't tell him what to do, either.) That response tells you that even when the child is obedient to his parents, down inside he is totally rebellious. He is not under any authority other than his own.

Granted, if the child perceived some devious intent on the part of a stranger who was attempting to abduct him, such independence would be in order. But don't delude yourself into being proud of your child's rebellion toward other adults as if she is expressing loyalty or acting in self-preservation. It is rebellion, which is as the *"sin of witchcraft"* (1 Sam. 15:23). Even when rebuked by another child, a properly trained child will see the rule of law behind the rebuke and come under subjection.

There is by nature in every child an innate awareness of his duty to conform to the common law of love and benevolence. This unwritten code is expressed when one small child says to another, "You ought not do that." The conscience that is not yet seared is constantly appealing for conformity to this innate standard. **When a child rebels against the just rebukes of his peers, he is not only rebelling against his peers, but against the "rule of law" in general.** The child need not be conscious of this "rule of law." Most adults aren't, but it unconsciously dominates our moral centers. For example, a child may not know what the word *rebellion* means, yet he will function exactly as an adult functions when in a state of rebellion. The child is violating his own conscience. He is suffering guilt. He is building a barrier of pride and self-love, and will become self-loathing. A child encouraged or permitted to continue thus is destined to moral destruction, and if left unchecked will shipwreck in this life, and eventually suffer eternal judgment.

THE OLDER SISTER

My two youngest daughters were nine and eleven years old when they were entertaining some children we were overseeing. A two-year-old girl picked up an item that was off limits. Her older sister, fourteen, told her she couldn't play with it and proceeded to take it away. The child threw a screaming fit. (That was her normal approach in paying back her parents.)

My nine-year-old, amazed at this bizarre behavior, came and told her mother. Upon investigating, Deb found the little girl was mad at her big sister for thwarting her heist. The younger girl felt that her older sister should have no jurisdiction over her behavior. The fourteen-year-old admitted she was not allowed to discipline her little sister. My wife immediately set up a training session. She took the forbidden object and placed it back on the floor in front of the child. "But that is tempting the child!" you say. Did not God do the same for Adam and Eve?

The child immediately stopped crying and in triumph looked at her sister and reached for the object. Deb said, "No, you can't have that." When the child grabbed it anyway, Deb said "No" and swatted her hand with a little switch. The child drew back, and Deb left the object within inches of the girl's grasp. Since the object was not out of reach, the child assumed it was still within limits. When she again reached, Deb gave her a spat and a calm command. After one or two more times, the child learned her lesson.

Deb then handed the object to the older sister and told her to place it in front of the child and tell her "No." As the fourteen-year-old laid the object close to the child, she reached out, only to jerk her hand back when told "No." The forbidden object was then left on the floor in the middle of the playroom. The little girl played around it the rest of the day without touching it. The child who had previously made everyone miserable by her demands was cheerful and congenial until it was time to leave. She had learned to respect the authority of her older sister and, by extension, the authority of anyone left in command.

KEEPING REBELLION ALIVE

To allow your child a time of rebellion and self-will (whether it is around your spouse, grandparents, older brothers or sisters, the babysitter, or his peers) is to allow rebellion and self-will to stay alive. The seeds of rebellion will always be there to come to fruition when the external pressures are lessened. You may be controlling his outward actions, but you are not building character.

In a family submitted to the light of God, children will be so surrendered to the unspoken principle of right conduct that they readily give and receive rebuke from one another. In the church, we are all accountable to one another. It should be so in the home. Furthermore, the older children will be more responsible when given responsibility over the younger children. And what a load it takes off the mother!

Though older children are placed in charge of the younger ones, the younger children are always allowed a court of appeal. If the older child abuses his or her authority, you should treat it as a grave offense. The younger children soon learn that to make an unfounded claim against the older child's discipline is to receive double discipline. The responsibility given to the older child is valuable training. It also lessens tensions since the older child is not left helpless in the presence of an unrestrained rioter.

In a home where only parents enforce obedience, siblings will never like each other, and older children will despise their little brothers and sisters. A practical arrangement is that when two kids are together, one should be in charge.

BLESSED MOTHER, HAVE MERCY

A number of times I have observed the difficult situation where one parent (usually the less-sentimental father) is firm in training for obedience, but the other parent (usually the mother, but not always) gives in to sympathy and is slack to demand and expect instant obedience. During the day while the father is away, the mother begs, nags, threatens, and after a while, becomes sufficiently angry to impress upon the children the need to yield temporary compliance.

The father comes home from work and is soon confronted with the rebellion and disobedience of his children. When he spanks the children, they wail cries of injustice. The emotionally weak mother so suffers from seeing her "babies being abused" by this "stranger" invading their domain that, in front of the children, she steps in to challenge his judgments. The children soon learn how to play the mother's emotions against the father's "justice." As the mother becomes more and more critical of the father and protective of the children, the children become liars and learn to manipulate the contentious adults.

The father sees he is losing control and bears down harder on the children. The mother, attempting to provide a balance, becomes even more permissive, and the gulf between them widens. Ties are broken, and the children suffer.

One parent should NEVER correct or question the other's judgment in the presence of the children, unless, of course, the actions rise to the level of criminal child abuse. It is better for your child if you support an occasional injustice than to destroy the authority base by open division. We see this manifested when a child who is being disciplined by the father begins to plead for his mother. When a child runs to the mother, the mother should take up the discipline as forcefully as the father would. If a father is attempting to make a child perform some act of obedience and the child cries for his mother, then the mother should respond by spanking the child for whining for her, and for his disobedience. He will then be glad to be dealing only with the father. He will never try to play one against the other again, unless, of course, he detects a lack of cohesion in the authority structure.

When we speak of administering a spanking in these circumstances, we are not advocating removing the child from the scene and making a big deal out of it. When the child has whined for his mother, she should go to him right where he sits in his high chair and give him one or two licks on his exposed ankles or legs while commanding, "Obey your father." You are not punishing the child; you are simply reinforcing your words and making clear your intentions to stick by your husband. You are training.

We broke this tendency of selective subjection early. When one of us was spanking one of the kids and they cried for the other parent, the other parent would come over and contribute to the spanking. After one or two times of that, the child decided that one parent was enough.

After a child has been spanked, he should not be allowed to flee to the other parent for sympathy. It is important that he find his solace in the one who did the spanking. When God chastens us, it is to draw us to Himself, not to cause us to turn to another. This is a profound issue to consider in your disciplining of children. After correcting a child for disobedience, command him to do something simple and inconsequential to put him back into the process of obedience. To immediately obey any command is a gesture of surrender.

Mother, if you think your husband is too forceful in his discipline, there is something you can do. While he is away, demand, expect, train for, and discipline the children to give you instant and complete obedience. When Father comes home, the house will be peaceful and well-ordered. The children will always obey their father, giving him no need to discipline them.

DEALING WITH ABUSE

If you think your spouse is abusive to the children, take these steps:

1. Sit down for a frank talk and express your concerns in a non-threatening way.

2. If your spouse becomes angry and refuses to consider the matter, go to a trusted friend who is wise and objective (not a gossip), or a church counselor, and share your concerns. Sometimes they can point you in a direction that will enable you to make changes that will cause your spouse to become more receptive to your concerns.

3. If that fails, inform your spouse that you can no longer tolerate the abuse and that you are going to begin taking it up the line to seek intervention.

4. Arrange for a counseling session at church with a wise individual, and then inform your spouse that he is to attend or you will be forced to take it to the authorities.

5. If your spouse refuses to seek counsel and continues the abuse, call the police and have him, or her, arrested for child endangerment.

Warning: If you are just seeking to end your marriage or punish your spouse and you exaggerate the situation, causing your spouse to face legal consequences, you are bearing false witness, which is to break one of the Ten Commandments—a grievous sin indeed.

CHAPTER 12

Training Examples

STRIKING OUT

As my wife was counseling with a young mother, I watched a most amazing scene unfold. A two-year-old boy, upon failing to get his mother's attention, picked up a plastic toy wrench and began to pound his mother's arm. Occasionally he would reach up and poke her in the face. This was not newly learned behavior. Previously, we had observed him follow in the footsteps of Cain as he perpetrated acts of violence on his little brother. Another time my wife saw him slamming a tricycle wheel down on his mother's foot. She cried out, "Johnny [the name has been changed to protect the guilty mother], that hurts Mother." And in a whining voice she added, "Don't hurt your Mother." Wham!! Down went the tricycle wheel on her foot again. "Stop it; that hurts!" Let me tell you what hurts. It hurts to see a mother abuse her child by doing nothing while her responses are making a criminal out of little Johnny.

Well, fortunately on this occasion it would turn out differently. As the talk continued, little Johnny got tired of assaulting his mother and turned on my wife. She was not his mother and was not "trained" to take his abuse, so without looking at him, and while the conversation continued unabated, Deb picked up a matching toy wrench and held it casually. She was preparing to teach the mother and the son a lesson. When little Johnny struck my wife again, without interrupting the conversation, and showing no anger or agitation, Deb returned the blow with more than matching force. Such surprise! What is that little pain Johnny feels coming from his arm? And somehow it is associated with the striking of this toy. Again, Johnny strikes. Again, swift reprisal (training is now in session). Johnny is very tough; so, although he didn't cry, he pulled back his pained arm and examined it carefully. You could see the little mental computer working. As if to test his new theory, again, but with less force, he struck once more. The immediately returned blow was not diminished in strength. This time, I thought surely he would cry. No, after looking at his mother as if to say, "What is this new thing?" he again, and with even less force, struck my wife on the arm. I was thinking, "She will lighten up this time and match his diminished intensity." Again, as if disinterested, my wife forcefully returned the blow.

Now, you may wonder what the mother was doing during this teaching exchange. Believe it or not, the two women continued to talk, my wife, as if all was normal, and the mother with a facial expression divided between wonder and mild alarm. Johnny, tough enough for Special Forces training, made one of those pained, crying faces, but covered it with a quick, forced smile. To my amazement, with about one-fourth the original force, he again struck my wife. Again, she returned the full-force blow. I was hoping that Johnny was getting close to learning his lesson. The conversation had about died in anticipation of the outcome. Johnny must have had a Viking lineage, for he continued to trade blows at least ten times. On Johnny's part, the blows got lighter and lighter until after a short, contemplative delay, he gave a little tap that was returned with a swift, strong blow. Finally, he let the toy wrench lie limp in his hand while he studied my wife's face. I think he was puzzled by her relaxed, non-aggressive expression. He was accustomed to being argued with and threatened. He had been trained to expect a growing level of antagonism preceding any actual confrontation. My wife never even spoke to him, hardly looked at him, and gave a friendly smile when she did.

Well, Johnny was a lot smarter than the cat that learned to keep his tail out from under the rocking chair. He turned away from my wife, shrugged his shoulders, bounced his legs, smiled, examined his arm, and looked at the wrench still in his hand. I could see an idea come into his experimental little head. He turned to his mother and forcefully pounded her on the arm. As she rubbed her arm and cried, "Johnneeeee, that hurrrrrt!" my wife handed her another toy wrench. The next time Johnny struck, the young mother courageously returned the blow. It only took two or three times to learn this lesson from his mother's hand. And *the mother was also being taught.* If she remained consistent, Johnny would be convinced that the world was not a passive punching bag.

Please understand that the use of the toy wrench was not a substitute for the rod. This was not discipline, but training. The child was cheerfully but aggressively striking with the toy, a behavior he had obviously practiced often at home. Though frustrated, he was not mean. Had that been the case, his medicine would have been a spanking. The returned blows were *teaching him* that what he was doing was painful and undesirable. He was also being taught that there were others who could give it out better than he. Meeting a bigger bully cures most little bullies. Children can learn not to pick up wasps by picking up only one.

Most people would find it hard to believe that this encounter actually endeared my wife to little Johnny. He seems to love her greatly and demands to be picked up when she is near. Children are comfortable around someone who has control of their own emotions and with whom they know their limitations. Since this experience, and with further counseling, both mother and child are showing great improvement.

Here we are twenty-three years later and the wrench whacker is now grown, with children of his own. He is not a bully and remains a good friend of the family.

LITTLE FOXES SPOIL THE VINES

We just returned from having supper with neighbors. They are a fine young couple who are just beginning their family. They are kind parents, concerned to rear their children properly. They would never be guilty of abuse or neglect. Their children are their priority. But as we sat talking I was once again reminded that it is often the little insignificant things that determine a child's character.

Their little three-year-old boy was between us, playing with a small, rubber bathtub goat. He apparently discovered there was still some water in it, so he held it over the table and began to squeeze. To the delight of everyone, and especially the boy, the goat began to relieve itself on the table. After a good laugh, the mother went to the kitchen for a towel.

When she attempted to wipe the table, the little fellow said "No" and tried to prevent her from removing his water puddle. She easily brushed him aside and wiped the puddle away. He gasped an angry and frustrated protest, then threw himself onto the couch and cried. The cry was not loud and did not last five seconds before he jerked around with protruded lip to see what other entertainment was available. It was all over in ten seconds.

The conversation resumed as he performed the first of a series of deliberate transgressions. He climbed onto the coffee table—which is always off limits—and then sought out other expressions of defiance. After about the fifth command, he would cease and go to the next escapade. The conversation continued with only an occasional lapse while his mother rebuked him. This is exactly the kind of issue that demands concentrated training and discipline. To ignore it as they did is to waste your child.

What did the child learn? He learned that his mother is bigger than he is and can force her will upon him. This justifies him enforcing his will upon his younger brother. He learned that he does not have to exercise self-control. Anything that he is big enough to achieve is fair game. The anger that was allowed to seethe in his heart led to rebellion. Though the parents were unaware of it, his subsequent actions were the product of his defiled heart.

THE PROPER RESPONSE

The proper response would have gone something like this: "Johnny, here is a rag. Please clean up your mess." "No, I don't wanna." He then continues to dabble in the water, sort of rocking back and forth with one shoulder and with his chin down, not too earnestly involved in the water, yet waiting to see if his mother is going to let him be. Rebellion is in his heart, but he faces a superior power, so he hesitates. Again she says, "Johnny, clean the water up, NOW." (With my children, one command is all they would get.) If he again hesitates, she goes for the switch. If he hurriedly attempts to avert a switching by cleaning up the water, it makes no difference. She returns with the switch, and standing in front of him, says, "Johnny I told you to wipe up the water, and you hesitated. Therefore I am going to have to spank you so you will not hesitate the next time. Mama wants her boy to grow up to be wise like Daddy, so I am going to help you remember to obey. Lean over the couch. Put your hands down. Now don't move or I will have to give you additional licks."

She then administers about five slow, patient swats to his bare legs. They are not hard and do not leave a mark, but he cries in pain. If he continues to show defiance by jerking around and defending himself or by expressing anger, then she will wait a moment and again lecture him and again spank him. When it is obvious that he is totally surrendered to her will, she will hand him the rag and very calmly say, "Johnny, clean up your mess." He should very contritely wipe up the water. To test and reinforce this moment of surrender, give him another command. "Johnny, go over and put all of your toys back in the box." Or, "Johnny, pick up all the dirty clothes and put them in the basket." After three or four faithfully performed acts of obedience, brag on how smart a helper he is. For the rest of the day, he will be happy and compliant. The transformation is unbelievable.

Therein lies the potential making of a peaceful home and of an emotionally stable and obedient child. If you are faithful to administer negative consequences upon every infraction, whether in attitude or action, in just a few days you will have a consistently obedient and cheerful child. The wonderful thing is that one act of obedience gained in a contest like this translates into a heart of obedience that will express itself positively in all future potential contests of will.

I DON'T HAVE THE TIME

Now, I know exactly what some of you are thinking. "But I am pushed to the limit now. I don't have the time to watch and guard against every transgression." **If you have duties outside the home that prevent you from properly rearing your children, give your duties back to the Devil.** I mean exactly that, even if they are church activities. If you have children, your first calling is that of a parent. If, on the other hand, you are overextended because of a chaotic household, then you cannot afford to do other than be faithful in training and discipline, for you desperately need the rest that well-trained children will provide.

Just yesterday, a young mother of small children came to the house and told my wife this story: "This morning, as I was sitting at the sewing machine, my four-year-old son came to me and said, 'Mother, I love you so much.' I stopped sewing, looked at the earnest expression on his face, and said, 'I'm glad you love me, for I love you too. You are such a fine boy.' As I attempted to turn back to sewing, he said, 'Do you know why I love you so much?' 'No, why do you love me so?' 'Because you make me bring in firewood and do what you say.'"

This mother always looks fresh and rested. Even a four-year-old can compare himself with other children and appreciate his parents' guidance.

A SWITCH AT NAPTIME SAVES MINE

When your baby is tired and sleepy enough to become irritable, don't reinforce his irritability by not addressing the cause. Put the little one to sleep.

I hate to see parents spank a kid for being grouchy when all he needs is sleep. But what about the grouchy child who would rather complain than sleep? Get tough. Be firm with him. Never put him down and then for some reason reverse your position, allowing him to get up. To maintain your position of authority, you *must* follow through. He may not be able to sleep, but he can be trained to lie there quietly. He will very quickly come to know that any time he is laid down there is no alternative but to stay put. To get up is to be on the firing line and get switched back down. It will become as easy as putting a rag doll to bed. Those who are MOSTLY consistent must use the switch more often—too often. Those who are ALWAYS consistent will quickly come to never need it.

When you first begin to train your child to lie down quietly, he may whimper and protest, which is just a natural expression of disappointment. If you ignore whimpering, it will pass. But if you reward the whimpering by letting him get up, he will repeat it the next time he wants to get up. Having discovered the power of whimpering, he will continue to employ it to get his way. By allowing the child to dictate policy, you are training him to be in charge. Since this whining and crying is eventually going to annoy Mother, it is better, regardless of the mother's feelings, to break this tendency before it takes root and becomes a habit. It is sickening to see grown men whine.

Just think of it, children who never beg, whine, or cry for anything! We have raised five whineless children. Think of the convenience of being able to lay your children down and say, "Naptime," and then lie down yourself, knowing that they will all be lying quietly in bed when you awake.

OBEDIENCE

As one mother was reading an early manuscript of this book, she became aware of the inappropriateness of her twelve-month-old daughter's whining. When she came to the part above about not allowing a child to whine, she decided to apply what she was reading. She put her daughter down and told her to go to sleep. The sleepy child responded by crying in protest. Following the book's instructions, she gave the child a couple swats with a little implement and told her to stop crying and go to sleep. This is not punishment; it is reinforcing your words. The child had previously been trained to spend an hour intermittently crying and getting up, only to be fussed at and laid back down. The unpleasant swats caused her to lie still. The mother continued her reading. After a while she looked up to see that the child had very quietly slipped to the floor to browse through a book. The mother smiled at how sweet and quiet the child was and continued reading the manuscript.

Reading further, she contemplated the fact that the child had not obeyed. "But she is being so good and is not bothering me," the mother thought. She then realized the issue was not whether the child was bothering her, but whether or not she was learning to obey. She rightly concluded that by allowing the child to quietly sit on the floor at the foot of her bed where she would eventually go to sleep, she was effectively training the child to disregard the rule of law. Out of love for her child, this mother inconvenienced herself and shattered the quiet solitude by spanking the child and again telling her to stay in the bed and go to sleep. The child went to sleep immediately.

THREE-YEAR-OLD MOTHER

The other day at our house, a three-year-old little girl was playing with dolls. (Let me interject: All children's dolls should be BABY dolls, not Barbie dolls. The fantasy arising from playing with baby dolls causes the child to role-play mother. The fantasy arising from Barbie dolls causes a child to role-play being a Playboy bunny. *"As [a child] thinketh in his heart, so is he"* [Prov. 23:7].) This little girl was role-playing mother. The thing that was interesting was the role this little "mother" assumed with her baby. In her imagination, the baby started crying after being given a command. She scolded her baby and then turned her over and spanked her. Then she spoke comforting, reassuring words and praised her baby for being good. She perfectly mimicked the loving, patient tone and firmness of her own mother.

As I continued to peek in at the proceedings, she continued her "mother" practice session. Several situations arose with her rag baby, which she promptly and firmly dealt with like an old pro. In fact, I could not have handled the make-believe situations any better. She told the screaming child (the rag doll), "No! That's not nice. You can't have it now. Stop your crying." SWITCH, SWITCH. "If you don't stop crying, Mama will have to spank you again." SWITCH, SWITCH, SWITCH. "Okay, stop crying now. That's better. Now see if you can play happily."

Here was a three-year-old "mother" already prepared to train up happy and obedient children. She knew exactly what to expect from her own mother. And what was even more amazing, she knew exactly what her mother expected from her. **She disciplined her baby doll for attitudes, not**

actions. This little three-year-old girl was completely trained. The battle was won. As long as her parents consistently maintain what they have already instilled, she will never be anything but a blessing.

BEGGARS CAN'T BE CHOOSERS

A child should NEVER whine or beg. This is an easy habit to break. **Never reward a beggar, and the begging will go away.** In our house, the one sure way of not getting your desire was to beg or whine. We went out of our way to not reward a begging child. If we had purchased a treat for the children and one of them became impatient and whined for it or asked twice, he was certain to be excluded, even if it meant that he was left to watch the other children eat the treat for which he had begged. If I was preparing to pick up a small child and he whined to be picked up, I would not pick him up until he became distracted and pleasant—even though it meant an inconvenience for me.

You may envision such a rule being enforced in your house producing a chorus of constant wailings of injustice. The very thought of it may make you feel like a tyrant. If you gave it a try, being 90% consistent, you would not be satisfied with the results. If a child ever gets his way through begging or whining, he will try it ten more times until it works again. And no amount of sporadic spanking will put a stop to it. But if his experience of begging *always* proves to be counterproductive, he will soon stop wasting his energy in fruitless whining. **When beggars can't choose, they choose not to beg.**

THE HARD WAY

For two years after the birth of our first child, my wife was unable to conceive. When she finally did, she had a miscarriage. Then one year later the little fellow whose name we had picked out five years earlier was finally born. Our first son! My wife was ever so possessive. By the age of one, he was so attached to her that I had to submit a request well in advance if I wanted to spend some time with her alone. He could not be left with a babysitter unless she was blessed with deafness. I didn't know much about children then, and thought this was just a "stage" that would run its course. Sound familiar? A friend who had more experience as a father was the one to show me otherwise.

I guess the men of the church had all they could take of this two-year-old with the umbilical cord still attached. My wife was the child's willing slave until that fateful day in April. I can still see my friend walking up to the car where we were unloading at a church outing. With the other conspirators shadowed in the background, he came up to my wife, reached out, swept Gabriel away, saying, "I'll take him," and was gone.

I couldn't understand what he wanted with that bucking, screaming, desperate kid who was reaching back over his shoulder pleading with his mother to rescue him. His accomplices closed in behind him as if to prevent any rescue. I supposed the misguided fellows would soon want to return him like one would want to return a cold to its donor.

To my wife it was the opposite of giving birth. She was being weaned. After a couple of hours the "trainers" came back around with a new Gabriel laughing and enjoying the men's company. He didn't run to his mother or resume his crying.

To our amazement, from that moment on the umbilical cord was dried up and we had a little boy whose world was larger than his mother's arms. Ha! And I had my wife back! The next boy was soon on the way, but he did not come to be an extension of his mother's self-image. We had learned our lesson.

AS THE WHEEL TURNS

When we babysit for other people, it is always on the condition that we be granted full liberty to discipline and train. We try to be realistic and use discretion in determining what can be effectively accomplished in the time allotted. We consider the child's trust in us, his or her acquaintance with our technique, the parents' sensitivity, and the child's emotional state.

On one occasion, Deb was keeping a mixed group of about ten children and babies, all from four different families attending a seminar. One couple's first child, about fifteen months old, was highly overindulged and showed it. He had been trained to expect constant catering and pacifying. He was missing his "mother-servant," and was complaining. It was not just the usual "I'm sad and lonesome; won't someone love me?" kind of whimpering. His crying said, "I'm mad as all get-out. Things are not going my way. Where is my mama anyway? I'm going to make everyone pay for this treatment. This will be a night they will not want to repeat. I'll see to it. Just try to stop me!"

Deb sat all the children at the table for a snack. After a couple of minutes, the little fellow began to pout. He didn't like the food or the company. He got down and began to complain. Giving him more leeway than we would have one of our own, my wife handed him a potato chip for which he had previously shown delight. True to his attitude, he defiantly threw it on the floor.

My ever-patient wife, who was also quite busy, picked him up and placed him in a big, soft chair, handing him a brightly colored roller skate. She took a moment to show him what fun it was to hold it upside down and turn the wheels. "See, turn the wheels," she said. With defiance, he turned his face away. This otherwise sweet child had developed (rather, the parents had trained into him) a selfish and rebellious spirit. If left to himself, he would *"[bring] his mother to shame."* My wife always had a special fondness for this child, and it hurt her to see him developing such a nasty attitude.

She decided it was showdown time. She ignored the other children, who were happily investigating and rearranging everything on the table, and quickly obtained her switch (twelve inches long and about the diameter of a small noodle). She again placed the skate in front of him and gently and playfully said, "Turn the wheels." Again, he defiantly turned his head away whimpering. She again demonstrated the fun of rolling the wheels and repeated the command. Again, defiance.

This time, being assured he fully understood it to be a command, she placed his hand on the wheels, repeated the command, and when no obedience followed, she administered one swift swat to his leg. This was not punishment or a full-fledge spanking; it was a training swat. It would not have been enough to cause a four-year-old to wince, but, although he did not cry, it was an irritant to the child. Again, in a mild but firm voice, she commanded him to turn the wheels. Self-will dies hard. My wife brought other children over to demonstrate the fun of wheel turning, all of them smiling and joyfully demonstrating the fun of spinning wheels. Pulling his hand as far from the skate as possible, he covered his right hand with his left—apparently to reinforce his resolve, or to demonstrate it—and refused to turn the wheels.

After about ten acts of stubborn defiance, each followed by one swat to the hand, he surrendered his will to one higher than himself. In rolling the wheels, he did what every human being must do—he humbled himself before the highest authority and admitted that his interests are not paramount. After one begrudged roll, my wife turned to other chores.

A few minutes later she noticed he was turning the wheels and laughing with the other children toward whom he had previously shown only disdain. The surly attitude was all gone. In its place was contentment, thankfulness, and a fellowship with his peers. The "rod" had lived up to its biblical promise.

Obviously, Deb was not concerned that the wheels on the skate got rolled. The task she urged upon him had no practical purpose other than training. She trained his mind to respect authority. She trained his will to accept discipline. The beautiful thing about a session like this is that it has ramifications for all areas of the child's life. The child has just one will, which, when it is surrendered to authority on any point, is always a surrendered will.

CHAPTER 13

Safety Training

Some training has nothing to do with character building. It just keeps your child alive and healthy. These illustrations may sound harsh or cruel to those living in a cloistered environment, but I have proven, along with many others, that this approach is both effective and safe.

GUN SAFETY

Being a hunting family, we have always had guns around the house. With our little ones, we made sure to keep the guns out of reach. But with the possibility of them sooner or later coming in contact with a loaded gun, we trained them to respect a gun as off limits.

With our first toddler, I placed an old, unused and empty, single-shot shotgun in the living room corner. After taking the toddlers through several "No" and hand-swatting sessions, they knew that guns were always off limits. Every day of their growing-up lives, they played around the gun without touching it. I never had to be concerned with their going into someone else's house and touching a gun. I did child-proof my guns, but I also gun-proofed my children.

HOT STOVE

We've always had a wood-burning stove for cooking and heating. A red-hot stove can seriously burn toddlers. I have seen some awful scars on other children. But we had no fear, knowing the effectiveness of training. When the first fires of fall were lit, I would coax the toddlers over to see the fascinating flames. Of course, they always wanted to touch, so I held them off until the stove got hot enough to inflict pain without burning, testing it with my own hand. When the heat was just right, I would open the door long enough for them to be attracted by the flames, and then I would close the door and move away. The child would inevitably run to the stove and touch it. Just as his hand touched the stove, I would say, "Hot!" It usually took just one time—twice with one child—but they all learned their lessons. We never had a child get burned. It was so effective that, thereafter, if I wanted to see them do a back flip, all I had to do was say, "Hot," and they would even drop a glass of iced tea.

SINKING FEELING

When our children were young, we had a pond in the immediate yard that served as a swimming pool and fishing hole. As they grew to be toddlers wandering around outside, we always watched them closely. Yet knowing the possibility of one getting out of sight, we cranked up the training. On a warm spring day I followed the first set of wobbly legs to the inviting water. She played around the edge until she found a way to get down the bank to the edge. I stood close by as she bent over, reaching into the mirror of shining color. Splash! In she went. I restrained my anxiety long enough for her to right herself in the cold water and show some recognition of her inability to breathe. When panic set in (mine as well as hers—not to mention her mother's), I pulled her out and scolded her for getting close to the pond. She didn't swallow any water, and there was no need for resuscitation—except on my wife, who took several hours to begin breathing normally. We repeated the same process with all the children. It only took one time for each of them to learn respect for the water. And it sure made life easier for us.

We did have trouble with Shalom. She is the one who became mobile early, crawling at four months and walking at seven. She always had marvelous coordination. She just wouldn't fall in. I got weary taking walks to the pond. So to bring the class to a timely graduation, I pushed. Oh, she didn't know it. As she was balanced over the water, I just nudged her with my foot. To this day I still believe that if I had left her alone, she would have been able to swim out. But it distressed her enough to make her not want to play close to the pond.

No, they didn't remain fearful of the water. My children were all swimming by the time they were four. We still watched them closely, and we never had a close call. *The training worked.* However, we do not recommend that you try this unless you are a good swimmer and are sure that you can maintain full control of all the circumstances. We offer these illustrations as a way to describe training, not as specific situations that you should mimic.

GET OUT FAST

One winter when my two younger girls were nine and eleven, they were riding with me in an old 4x4 Army truck. The gravel road was bumpy and rough. When I made a stop at an intersection, I heard the two 12-volt batteries, located right behind the seats, short out and begin to arc. An explosion of spraying battery acid was potentially imminent. The girls understood none of this. However, when I commanded (this time in a raised voice), "Get out fast!" they didn't ask, "Why?" I immediately got out on my side to run around and open their usually jammed door. As soon as I cleared the door on my side, I looked over my shoulder to see how they were doing. They were gone. The door was still closed, and the window, which also sticks, was only open about halfway. But they were nowhere in sight. When I got around to the other side, there they were piled up on the gravel road rubbing scuffed hands and knees—a drop of five feet. "How did you get out?" I asked. "Through the window," they choked out. "Head first?" I asked. "You said get out fast!" was their accusing reply.

My son, who was driving another truck behind me, said, "I didn't know what was happening. Suddenly they both came flying out the window head first and landed in the road." I had trained them to jump upon command, and they did. There may come a time when their safety or survival will depend on instant obedience. "Duck!" or "Hit the deck!" has saved more than one life.

TRAIN FOR REALITY

The world is sometimes a hostile place. A child must learn to take precautions early. Don't give your children a modified sense of reality. Teach them about heights and falling, about guns, the danger of knives and scissors, the caution of sharp sticks and coat-hanger wires, the terror of fire, and the danger of poisons and electricity. School them. Drill them. Show them examples. Expose them to death—the death of a pet or an accident victim. This must be done with calm, confident reverence, not with fear. Don't be excessive. One or two examples to a three-year-old are enough.

It's okay to control their environment, but don't shut out reality. Expose them to it at a level they can comprehend and at a rate suitable to their maturity. The goal is to keep the training ahead of any external, threatening assaults and to have them worldly-wise by the time they must face it on their own.

SNAP TO IT!

I am the general. My wife is my aide and advisor—the first in command when I am absent. I rule benevolently. **Love and respect are my primary tools of persuasion.** I lead, not command from a distant bunker. All of my family know that I will lay down my life for them; consequently, they will lay down theirs for me. They find joy and pride in being part of the team. To instantly obey a command is their part of the teamwork. In doing so, the home runs smoothly and our common objectives are met.

I have taught the children to obey first and ask questions later. By putting them through paces when they were small, they learned to immediately do what I said. If they ever failed to instantly obey a command, I would drill them. "Sit down," I would say. "Don't speak until I tell you to." Understand, I was not taking out my frustrations on them. It was all done with utmost pleasantness. "Stand up," I would command. "Now, come here. Go touch the door." And, before they could get there, "Sit." Plop, down they would go. "Now, go to your rooms and clean them up." Just like little, proud soldiers, off they would go to the task. They thought it was just a fun game, but it drilled into them instant obedience.

If one of them should fail in his attitude, which wasn't very often, he would be spanked—without haste or hostility, mind you. Childish negligence or clumsiness was a time for patience and grace, whereas rebellion was an occasion for corporal chastisement.

This may sound cold and harsh. I hope it doesn't, for it was warm, friendly, and loving, and produced five confident, calm, hard-working, loyal children and adults. In actuality, *because of our consistency* in this method of training, the children were seldom spanked. They all soon learned that every transgression received a *"just recompense of reward."* They knew that, without a doubt, delayed obedience meant a meeting with the rod. Delayed obedience was dealt with as disobedience. Firmness with consistency gives the children a great sense of security.

Even today, without looking at the children, I can snap my finger, pointing to the floor, and they all (including the ones over six feet) immediately sit. I can point to the door, and they all exit. When a visit develops into a counseling session, I have given the gesture for the children to vacate the room, and our company never knew what prompted everyone to leave. Teach your children to "snap to it." They will be better for it, and it will make them more lovable—which makes for more loving all around.

CHAPTER 14

Potty Untraining

NO MORE DIAPERS

On a missionary trip to Central America, we were amazed by the practice of the primitive Maya Indians in not diapering their babies prior to stuffing them into a carrying pouch. Their infants were all potty trained. After experimenting on our own and with further observation, we discovered that infants, like many mammals, are born with an aversion to going in their "nests." Parents here in the States "untrain" them by forcing them to become accustomed to going in their clothes. A child instinctively protests a bowel movement. He kicks, stiffens, and complains. Being sensitive to the warning signs (after having changed 17,316 diapers with the first four), my wife tried it on our new arrival.

When she sensed that Shoshanna was about to "go," she rushed her to the toilet and placed the infant against her bare legs in a spread-leg, sitting position. Dribbling a little stream of warm water over the child's private parts aided the start of an impending tinkle. As the child began urinating, Deb would say, "Pee-pee." On other occasions if she missed the signs and a bowel movement was in progress, Deb would rush the child to the bathroom to finish on the toilet, while occasionally saying, "Doo-doo." Even if the child was through with her elimination, Deb still sat her on the toilet in order to reinforce the training. The infant came to identify the sound of the words with the muscle function. She became so well trained to the voice command that we had to be careful not to say the words at the wrong time. We could be bragging to our neighbor, say the magic words, and possibly induce a release.

Now, some disbelieving mothers have said, "*You* are the one who is potty trained, not the baby." Just as a mother knows when her baby is hungry or sleepy, she can also tell if she needs to go potty. A three-week-old baby is doing all she can to communicate. Yes, Mother must be trained to listen. That is part of the job description.

My mother-in-law was equally skeptical until the day my wife said to her, "Stop at the next service station, the baby wants to go potty." They stopped, and as Deb came out with a thoroughly relieved three-month-old, my mother-in-law became a believer. For a while, our bathroom became the end of a pilgrimage for those seeking faith in infant potty training. Many a time our red-faced, infant girls looked up to see a great cloud of amazed witnesses expectantly hovering above them in our large bathroom.

Understand, the child is not *made* to sit for long periods of time waiting to potty. There is no discomfort for the child. An infant soon becomes accustomed to being regulated to about every two hours, or according to sleeping and eating intervals. Many others have also been successful in training their infants with this method.

But one note of caution: Potty training is not a matter of character training. If you fail to train an infant, don't let it bother you. You will be bothered enough when you change all the stinky diapers, pay to have your carpet shampooed, and replace the back seat of your minivan. You are not a bad parent if you don't potty train your infant early.

A HOSE WHEN HE GOES

A good friend and neighbor had a big three-year-old boy who would sit outside driving nails with a hammer and dumping in his diaper. I suggested it was time to have a man-to-man talk with the kid about the environmental implications of making such large contributions of plastic and paper to the city dump. The father, a college graduate, explained that he did not want to cause guilt or stifle the young man's personality. I well understood his concerns, for I have seen many distraught, impatient parents doing emotional damage to their children through verbal abuse over this very personal matter. So I suggested a training exercise.

First, I pointed out that the boy's mother, busy with the other children, would pick up this big kid several times a day, talk sweetly to him, lay him on a bed, take off the dirty diaper, wipe him with a warm, damp cloth, rub a little lotion on the chaffed spots, and then put a fresh, smooth diaper on him. Dumping in his pants had become an opportunity to get his mother's undivided attention. Now, understand that there is no guilt or blame in this matter, especially on the child's part, but there is something quite inconvenient—except for the kid who loved the experience and must have found it the highlight of his day.

Next, I suggested to the father that he explain to the boy that "Now that he is a man, he will no longer be washed in the house. He is too big and too stinky to be cleaned with the baby wipes. From now on, he will be washed outside with a garden hose." The child was not to be blamed. I suggested he communicate to the child that this is not punishment, rather a progressive change in methods—the final stage before he starts using the toilet like a man.

The next time the boy loaded down his diaper, the father took him out and merrily, and might I say, carelessly, washed him off. With the autumn chill, about 65 degrees, and the cold well water, I don't remember if it took a second washing or not, but a week later the father told me his son was now taking himself to the potty. The child weighed the alternatives and opted to change his lifestyle. Since then, many others have been the recipients of my meddling, and it usually takes no more than three cheerful washings. In the winter, you will have to modify your methods and wash him in the shower or tub. Just make sure it is not a rewarding experience for the child.

MANY SWEET RETURNS

One little three-year-old diaper dumper, looking rather shocked when watered down with the hose, gritted his teeth, and adjusted to the inconvenience. When it became clear to his parents that they had a tough, resolute martyr on their hands, they sought another solution. The mother realized that since this was her last child, she just hadn't wanted the little fellow to grow up. He enjoyed being the baby as much as she enjoyed it.

These parents, conscious of their children's nutritional needs, served them very few sweets. On rare occasions when they did, it was a real treat. This little fellow was a Spartan when it came to bodily discomforts, but he sure did love the sweets. The wise mother cheerfully said to the boy, "Son, Mother has decided that you are just not old enough to be eating sweets, so until you get a little bigger and stop messing in your clothes, you will not be allowed anything sweet."

For a week he seemed to be as monkish about the sweets as he was the hose. Then the day for french toast came around. Not eating syrup, they were allowed one teaspoon of powdered sugar per toast. After watching the older children receive their powdered sugar, the forlorn fellow said to Mama, "I sure do like powdered sugar on my french toast." "I know you do," she said, "but you are not old enough yet." After his deprived breakfast of plain french toast, he climbed down, walked around to his mother, and with all the soberness of one making a revolutionary, life-changing decision, he announced, "Mother, I am ready to stop wearing a diaper. Take it off." That was it. From that moment on he took himself to the toilet. A week later the little man, no longer wearing a diaper, climbed up to the table and had his french toast crowned with a spoonful of powdered sugar.

A NOTE OF WARNING

Bed-wetting or diaper dumping is not a moral or character issue. It is a natural, physical function. Don't let your pride do damage to your child. No matter how ashamed or embarrassed you might be, don't apply emotional pressure on your little ones. They are the product of your training and conditioning.

If you have an older child who wets the bed in his sleep, understand that it is not a conscious act that can be corrected by the methods mentioned above; nor is it an attitude problem that can be dealt with by discipline. The problem may be physical or emotional. Regardless, buy yourself a set of plastic sheets and teach the kid to change his own bed covers. Never embarrass him or cause him to feel blame.

If you suspect it could be emotional, examine your family and see if you can discover the cause. The child will grow and mature more happily in an atmosphere of deep love and respect.

CHAPTER 15

Child Labor

WORK DETAIL

"It's easier for me to do it," is a common reply. Another mother says, "But I feel guilty making them work; that's my job." One area in which our family was weak with the first children was the work detail. The children were, of course, given jobs here and there, but we failed to hold them responsible to a daily work detail. If I were doing it over again, this area of child training would get much more attention. In the early years, the mother is primarily responsible for this training. Simply put, when a child is old enough to take a toy out of a box, he is old enough to put it back.

Mother, let your time of interaction always be training. It is natural and can actually be fun. Instead of just playing, "I'm going to get you," play, "Here's how we put our toys away. See, I put one in, now you put one in. That's good. You're a smart boy, and you help Mama so much." Keep the chores within the scope of their concentration. Too much will weary them; too little will prevent it from being meaningful. It is your responsibility to make sure the children do not feel like slaves when they work. Kids hate to work alone. If their experience is so boring that they just wilt, then do not keep pushing; stop what you are doing and work with them. Conversation while working turns work into fellowship.

When they are under five, it takes more time to be their "employer" than to be their servant, but the best time to establish lifelong habits is before this age. By the time they are four or five, they should feel not just wanted, but needed. My Amish neighbors say that before seven the children are a drain on the family—costing money and time. Between seven and fourteen, they pay their way. After fourteen, they become an asset, bringing in profit. Certainly by the time a child reaches seven, he should be making your life easier. A houseful of seven-year-olds could easily be self-sustaining.

It is essential to a child's self-image that he feels the value of his contribution. Though he may show a reluctance to work, he is happier when his participation is significant. Mother, if you take a little time to train when they are young, you will be able to rest more when they are older.

I have observed many families train their first child to be responsible and work hard, especially if the first child is a girl, but as the other children come along, mother fails to train them because the firstborn is able to handle all the chores so efficiently. The idleness of the younger children causes them to develop low self-esteem, and they may fight with each other out of boredom. Not being taught to work when they were two and three, they resent being made to work when they are six and seven. "That is Big Sister's job, not mine. I am supposed to just stay out of the way and play." When you have six children it is hard to take the time to involve the little ones in work that could be quickly done by older children, but our goal is not to get the work done; it is to train up every child in the way he should go.

Teach them to clean up all their own messes, and they will make fewer messes. Divide the household chores among them according to their sizes and abilities. A child working below his ability will be bored and discontent. A child challenged will be cheerful. Don't pay or bribe a child to work. An exception should be made where the work is not routine household chores. When an outside job is taken on for income, they can share in the profits in realistic proportion to their work. Don't overpay a child, for it does not reflect the real world and will tend to leave them dissatisfied when they are eventually paid no more than they are worth.

A mother should always keep in mind that she is molding her daughters into future wives and mothers. Challenge them with sewing, cooking, cleaning, and learning about every aspect of household management. Let them get their hands in the dough (unless the child-training teacher is coming for dinner). From the time they are big enough to tell a tale, it should be natural to hear them talking about "what Mama and I did today."

Fathers, by the time the boys can follow you around they should be "helping" you work. My boys were climbing through sawdust and stumbling over briars before they could see over the tops of my boots. They were bringing firewood in when they were so young that they had to team up to roll it through the door. If you leave your sons for the women to rear, don't be surprised if at sixteen they act more like daughters.

Years ago, passing a neighbor's house, we observed an interesting scene. The father was patiently standing over his two boys (one and two years old) instructing them as they folded a tarp. The little one-year-old's wobbly fat legs were held apart by a sagging diaper that obviously needed changing. But he was working, on his way to being Daddy's man. Twenty years later those two young men are the hardest working young husbands around. They are both highly skilled in manly arts and are prospering financially, well beyond their years.

When families were part of a larger family unit, or even when the boys were in public school, the absence of a father role model was less significant. Where a working father leaves his boys with a flock of girls to be homeschooled by their mother, they often lack important traits of masculinity acquired only from working with men. I have seen notable exceptions. The mother provides outside work and play activities where the boys can do boy things and are not subject to the emotions and society of the girls.

Gender-role distinction is demeaned in modern education. The public and private schools today lack the masculinity of fifty years ago. They are filled with girly boys and most of the few male teachers that exist are leftists. Don't let a coven of sodomites and socialists hiding behind the badge of "professional psychology" reprogram your natural understanding of male and female distinctiveness. **A boy needs a man's example if he is to grow up to be a man.** If you are a single mother, find a godly Christian man who will mentor your sons. Make sure he is not a pervert. If your kids can play with other boys who have a wholesome relationship with their fathers, that will be a big help as well.

WIFE, WOULD YOU SAY A WORD? (BY DEBI PEARL)

One of the most important aspects of child training is letting a child take on real responsibilities. Children need to see that their contribution to the running of the household is vital. Training along these lines eliminates the fighting and fussing over chores when the children get older. Spend a few minutes with each child every day going over different chores step by step. When our second daughter was seven years old, she needed a job that required diligence, so I delegated to her the responsibility of keeping up the main bathroom. She not only kept it clean, she was responsible for seeing that it was supplied with all the necessary toiletries.

When the time came for our oldest daughter to go off to Bible college, she called her nine- and eleven-year-old sisters in and passed on to them her responsibilities. As I watched her train them in the various chores, which included laundry, cooking, and kitchen clean-up, I knew I had done something right. It was a change of command, a very sober and thrilling occasion for the younger girls. To the older, departing sister it was a day of great pride to be able to entrust the younger girls with her responsibilities. Over the next year, I watched as the two younger sisters, with great dignity, assumed all her household duties.

Although I am still the mom, they are *my* next-in-command. I have often come home tired from a stressful counseling session to find dinner cooked, the house clean, the clothes washed, and two grinning girls doing a silly bow as I walked through the door. Many a time, after spending a long morning in the living room encouraging an overworked, overextended, exhausted mother, we would hear a cheerful call from the kitchen. The table would be lined with small children already eating, and a good lunch would be set for us moms. An occasion like that does more to persuade a mother to train her children than all the teaching I could ever give. For every minute you spend in training your child, you are rewarded a hundredfold.

Our sons learned several trades before they were fourteen. They could farm, work in construction, log, hunt herbs, and cut hickory for sale to furniture manufacturers. They love working. The discipline learned in work translates into discipline in studies and, later, discipline in life. *No one is educated who cannot endure the routine of work.* There is a certain confidence that can only be obtained through the successful labor of your hands.

Recently, there was a death among one of the Mennonite families in our community. Several of the grown brothers and sisters came back to bury their beloved brother. All of these siblings were raised with the same hard work, careful discipline, and only an eighth-grade Mennonite education. In the pine box under the apple tree outside the old church house lay a farmer who probably never made more than two or three thousand dollars a year.

The five brothers looking on seemed out of place in this primitive setting. One is a neurosurgeon, another is a lawyer, one is a city planner, and another is a computer scientist. The fifth one has also gone on to be successful in life; he is a happily married Mennonite farmer. If you consider the first four successful, know that it was not early educational opportunities or special privileges that gave them the advantage. It was the confidence and ambition that comes from hard work and careful discipline in a family setting.

CHAPTER 16

Attitude Training

KEEPING LITTLE HEARTS

The attitude of your children is far more important than their actions or education. When a child has an innocent heart, clumsiness or misjudgment can be accepted as perfection.

For instance, one mother left her little girl doing minor housework. She returned to find that the little girl had voluntarily expanded her role. She had brought in the clothes from off the line, then folded and put them away. The only problem was that some of the clothes were still damp. This mother, seeing the proud glow in her little girl's eyes, accepted the offering as perfect. It was not until after the little helper had gone out to play that Mother removed the damp clothes and returned them to the line. She *later* trained her little daughter to know the difference between wet and dry clothes.

Training certainly must consider the actions, but **discipline should be concerned only with the child's attitude.** It is embarrassing to see a parent upset at a child for spilling milk or acting his normal, clumsy self. Judge them as God judges us—by the heart.

On the other hand, there are times when there is no disobedience, but the attitude is completely rotten. Parents must be on guard to discern attitudes. If we wait until actions become annoying before initiating discipline, we are only dealing with the symptoms. The root of all sin is in the heart. Know your child's heart and guard it. *"Keep thy heart with all diligence; for out of it are the issues of life"* (Prov. 4:23). It will be several years before your child can *"keep"* his own heart; until then, it is entrusted to you. Let us consider some real-life examples.

SURLY TEEN

A very frazzled mother of several children, who sometimes appears as emotionally worn out as an old Confederate flag, confided with me on her failures with her thirteen-year-old daughter. The girl, when asked to change a diaper on one of the small children, curled her lip in a surly manner and looked at her mother as if to say, "Why do you do this to me?" The mother accepted the response as added weight to her already-heavy load in life. After the daughter was out of hearing, the mother resignedly said, "My daughter is going to have to answer to God for herself. For a while I felt guilty, like my sins were being reflected in my daughter; but (and her voice trailed off for lack of certainty) she will have to find God for herself."

This mother has several young children and a dread of any more on the way. With all the responsibilities of homeschooling and natural living, she is too emotionally taxed to maintain responsibility for one as old as thirteen. It was as if she was giving up on this one to pour what strength she had left into the ones coming on.

Hard work is never as draining as tension. One who is emotionally discouraged wakes up tired. The thirteen-year-old daughter, who should be a blessing and encouragement to her mother, is an added burden. If this older daughter had been given proper attitude training, the mother would not be vexed now.

It is not impossible—although it is much more difficult—to alter the attitude of older children. They reach a point where appeal and reason are a parent's only recourse. When a child gets old enough to possess the reins of his own heart, he must be wooed as a sinner is wooed by the Holy Spirit.

STARTING OVER

Those of you who have stair-step kids in a dismal state of disorder may be discouraged with the seeming impossibility of retraining the whole lot. Take heart; *it can be done!* Start with the young children—the ones still within an age range to show quick improvement. Be *absolutely* consistent, and don't let the older ones discourage you. Their time is coming!

There is a wonderful psychological principle working for you. When an occupying military restores calm to a district previously in a state of anarchy, the other districts take notice and voluntarily quiet down. Confess to your older children that you failed to properly train them; accept the blame. But now that you know better, you are going to do things differently with the younger children. The older, unruly kids will sit back and watch. When they see the least improvement in their spoiled little brothers and sisters, they will be on your side—though they may not say so. When they become convinced of an absolutely positive transformation in the younger siblings and see the resulting fellowship and goodwill, they will want to get on the reclamation list. As long as you remain compassionate, sane, benevolent, *and consistent,* they will submit to your discipline, seeing and believing it to be for their own good.

When times of anarchy do occur, your control will carry them through until their emotions settle and they can view things more objectively. When you reclaim one, the others will know where you are headed and will be confident that you mean business. When you pen up dogs, horses, or cows, they will run around searching until they are sure there is no way out and then they will settle down. Once you convince a child that there is no alternative, he will submit.

Your children's natural self-love causes them to adopt the easiest position in any given circumstance. They love themselves too much to buck the inevitable. But remember, they know you presently as a vacillating weakling, never sticking by your principles, ignoring them when it would be inconvenient to do otherwise. So they will try to make your change of resolve very uncomfortable. Start with the youngest and work your way up. Let them know what is coming. Grin, because you have secret weapons: a plan, love, patience, reproof, THE ROD OF CORRECTION, endurance, and the hope of reward as promised in the Scripture.

THROWING A FIT—TEMPER TANTRUMS

My nine- and eleven-year-old daughters came in from a neighbor's house complaining of a young mother's failure to train her child. A seven-month-old boy who failed to get his way had stiffened, clenched his fists, bared his toothless gums, and called down damnation on the whole place. His expression resembled someone instigating a riot. The young mother, wanting to do the right thing, stood there in helpless consternation, apologetically shrugged her shoulders, and explained her helplessness by saying, "What can I do?" My incredulous nine-year-old answered, "Switch him." The mother responded, "I can't; he's too little." With the wisdom of a veteran who had been on the receiving end of the switch, my daughter answered, "If he is old enough to pitch a fit, he is old enough to be switched."

PERSISTENCE

Some struggling parents have asked, "But what if the child only screams louder and gets madder?" You have to realize that if he is accustomed to getting his unrestricted way, you can expect just such a response once, maybe even three times. He will simply continue to do what he has always done to get his way. It is his purpose to intimidate you and make you feel like an overbearing tyrant. Don't be bullied. Give him more of the same. Switch him eight or ten times on his bare legs or bottom. Then, while waiting five minutes for him to calm down, speak calm but firm words explaining what you expect and assuring him of your commitment to that end. If you hear the defiance go out of his cry, you know that he has given up his stubbornness and surrendered to your authority. But if his crying is still defiant and protesting, talk to him until he calms down enough so that you have his attention and then spank him again. If this is the first time he has come up against someone more determined than he is, it may take a while. If you must spank him more than twice, you will need to lighten up on the licks. The certainty of a spanking is what makes it effective, not the severity. He must be convinced that you have truly altered your expectations and will settle for nothing less than total obedience.

If you stop the process before the child is voluntarily submissive, you have confirmed to him the value and effectiveness of screaming in protest. The next time it will take twice as long to convince him of your commitment to his obedience because he will have learned the ultimate triumph of endurance in this episode in which he has prevailed. Once he learns that the reward of a tantrum is a swift spanking and a denial of his demands, he will NEVER throw another fit. It is not in his interests to do so. If you enforce the rule three times and then fail on the fourth, he will keep looking for that loophole until you have convincingly persuaded him that *it will not work again!* You can't train him if you are not consistent.

If a parent starts early, discouraging the first crying demands, the child will never develop the habit. In our home, a fit was totally unknown, because the first time it was tried, we made it counterproductive.

There is no justification for this to ever be done in anger. If you are the least bit angry, wait until another time. Some parents are so guilt-laden and embarrassed that they are unable to carry this through with calm resolve.

Please take note, the scenario we described is not to be the normal way of life. It is that one-time, initial conquering of a child who has not been trained and has decided to test your resolve. And if you do not conquer his will after several spankings, do not continue to spank. If spanking is unproductive, then you are involved in an exceptional situation. When spanking doesn't work, you need to get some counsel from a likeminded parent who has been successful. Ask them to observe and critique your parenting methods. They may be able to see something you are missing.

PARENTAL PROTOTYPES

Never expect more of your children's attitudes than the attitudes you display. In a situation where one or both of the parents are an emotional wreck, not much can be expected from the child. **A CHILD IS GOING TO BE THE HARVEST OF HIS PARENTS' TEMPERAMENTS.** If the mother is sulky, critical, or selfish, the children will have a tendency to be the same. If the father is a bully or full of anger and impatience, his sons will be too; or his sons may be broken in spirit and lack confidence. If the father is rude, demanding, and disrespectful of the mother, you can expect the same from his sons. If a father is intemperate or lustful, the children will likely be worse. I have seen many children openly despise their parents' sins, yet grow up to be just like them.

The lesson is this: **YOU MUST BE what you want your child to be—in attitude as well as actions.** Don't try to "beat the ugly" out of a child who is simply a display window of your own heart attitudes. An ounce of example is worth a pound of instruction.

THEY BETTER NOT MISTREAT MY BABY

A common problem more often found in mothers is the "They better not mistreat my baby" syndrome. I can still remember, when I was young, looking on with disgust as some swaggering brat sneered out of one side of his mouth and threatened to tell his mother. How did his parents produce such ugliness in him?

It's easy. Just be very protective of your child and always get emotionally involved in his disputes with other children. Let him see your anger when he is "mistreated" by his peers, babysitters, teachers, or other adults. Let him know you believe he is always in the right and that people are out to mistreat him, but you are there to see he gets his due. And to cap it off, when someone who is the child's senior comes to you with an accusation against your child, respond by accusing that person of lying. When your child knows that he can control any social relationship through his deceit and threats, and that you will never believe the accusation against him, you are breeding a very ugly temperament.

It is not going to harm your child to be falsely accused a few times (that's life). He must learn to deal with it sooner or later. When he is accused, if you have doubts about his guilt, patiently search out the matter. If you determine that he has been falsely accused, tell him, and then quietly drop the subject. Don't let him see your defensiveness on his behalf.

If he is roughed up by his peers, rejoice; he is learning early about the real world. Don't make a sissy out of him. If you jump to his defense every time another child takes away a toy, pushes him down, or even pops him in the nose, you will produce a social crybaby.

When you demand that your child be treated fairly, you are protecting him from reality. The younger they are, the easier it is for them to learn that they deserve no special treatment. Your reactions are not going to make life any less unfair for your child, but there is a danger of stirring up a feel-sorry-for-myself attitude in him. If you are tough, he will be tough. If you are joyful, he will be joyful as well.

If you live in a community where bullying is a way of life and your child is the butt of most of the bull, it may be too much for him to handle without joining a gang for mutual protection. If that is the case, then move into a community where your children are confronted with a normal amount of conflict.

WHY IS EVERYBODY ALWAYS PICKING ON ME?

While I taught a Bible class, my two daughters helped babysit a house full of children under five years old (five children under five is indeed a house full). One of the mothers returned to find her three-year-old daughter whining from being mistreated by a little fellow under two. They all confirmed that the stumbling toddler had in fact provoked a class-A altercation without sufficient provocation. The older and physically superior little girl just sat on the floor and "turned the other cheek"—only to have it walloped also. In her presence, the mother pitied the little girl and spoke critically of her assailant.

My daughters watched the situation carefully, and on several occasions observed him assaulting her. But as the nursery workers cracked down on the mugger, he ceased his misdemeanors. (Most of the "attacks" were actually the result of his stumbling while practicing his recently acquired skill of walking.)

The bright and otherwise sweet little girl was very obedient, but she had developed a habit of exhibiting emotional weakness in order to get her way. She whined about everything and seemed to suffer out of proportion to her happy lot in life. The young mother had cultivated this tendency.

During the succeeding weeks, the mother would greet her daughter with a sympathetic inquiry as to her suffering at the hands of the twenty-four-inch nursery stalker. The nursery workers became aware that the "victim" always gave an evil report. They made it a point to watch closely and were sure that on the occasions when there was no conflict with the alleged assailant, the little girl still gave a report of being attacked. They observed her playing happily until the mother arrived, at which time she would jump up and run into the arms of her sympathetic mother with whining tales of abuse.

As the talk escalated and the stumbling tot's infamy grew, the mother more carefully questioned her daughter. It was becoming clear that the emotionally weak child thrived on playing the role of the abused.

One night, the babysitters observed the little girl telling the boy, "Hit me. Go on, hit me." When she finally persuaded him to reach out and lightly strike her on the head, she went to one of the childcare workers crying about being struck. This was repeated on several occasions. Then, when the protective mother arrived, the little girl had a tale of abuse to again make her the center of her mother's sympathy.

On another occasion, when the little fellow was in the other room, the girl fell down, crying of being struck by him. When the mother arrived and those in charge told her that her daughter lied about being abused, she again took up the child's defense and denied that her daughter could lie.

I rejoice to say that this mother is one of the most teachable women I have ever met. When confronted, the mother realized she was making provision for her daughter to grow up breaking the ninth commandment: *"Thou shalt not bear false witness against thy neighbor"* (Ex. 20:16). She also realized she was cultivating a sour disposition in her little girl. She repented and immediately began working on it. When the child discovered that her pitiful complaints of abuse were met with skepticism and emotional distance, she stopped propagating her lies and employed legitimate means to gain attention.

BAD ATTITUDE

Bad attitude is bad through and through. For as a child *"thinketh in his heart, so is he"* (Prov. 23:7). *"Keep thy heart with all diligence; for out of it are the issues of life"* (Prov. 4:23). If a child shows the least displeasure in response to a command or duty, you should treat it as disobedience. If a child sticks out his lip, you should focus your training on his bad attitude. A wrong slant of the shoulders can reveal a bad frame of mind. Consider this a sign to instruct, train, or discipline. A cheerful, compliant spirit is the norm. Anything else is a sign of trouble.

If your family has always been out of control, to even consider training your children in this manner may seem overbearing and unrealistic. Granted, if some families simply started demanding this level of obedience, they would indeed be overbearing. But when approached as a revamping of the entire family, it no longer appears unreasonable. Sulking, pouting, whining, complaining, begging, and the like should ALL be eradicated like a bad disease. *Clean the whole house!*

This is not just an idealistic goal that we entertain while secretly being willing to settle for far less. It is the daily experience of multitudes of families, including our own. Like any well-cared-for garden, weeds do come up that must be dealt with, *but they are never given a chance to seed.* Problems do arise, but the training base we have described provides the certainty of a thriving garden of happy, satisfied children.

CHAPTER 17

Emotional Control

THE AMISH FAMILY

When an Amish family comes over to visit, bringing their twelve children, they are as quiet and orderly as a Japanese delegation visiting the Capitol building for the first time. They teach their children to maintain control of their emotions and always be respectful of our property and presence. When in the company of adults, the children don't talk or play loudly. If hurt, they don't cry excessively. The children learn to "give over" when another child tramples on their rights. Consistent training and discipline is the key to this kind of order.

SCREAMING TEEN

On one of those Sunday afternoons when the church was having dinner on the grounds (This is not eating off the ground; It is eating together outdoors.), a twelve-year-old girl who had been swinging on a swing set commenced to scream the cry of the imminently perishing. If one of my kids had screamed like that, I would have expected her to be caught in a people-eating machine, slowly being dragged to destruction. We all threw our paper plates of food on the ground and ran to the rescue. She appeared to have fallen out of the swing, but with no perceptible damage. (We later discovered what had precipitated the fall: she had received one bee sting.) When the father tried to examine her for what he thought was a broken arm, she rolled and thrashed, kicked and squalled. She sounded much like someone tied to a hill of fire ants.

For the next ten minutes her father continued trying to get her attention, demanding to know what was wrong. She wouldn't let him perform an examination, but continued screaming. After ten seconds of that, I said to my wife, "She isn't hurt, she's mad."

As I returned to find my paper plate, I could occasionally hear the father's bellow over hers, "What's wrong, honey? Tell me where it hurts." I knew she wasn't hurt badly, for no one who was truly hurt could muster that much energy for so long. Furthermore, the screaming had the sound of a protest— an assault cry.

After the men had shared a couple more fishing tales, we saw them carry her past us into the house, where her arm was eventually pronounced just fine. I was glad when they finally got her indoors. With all the background noise, the men were starting to tell violent stories of war and conflict. Take care not to make emotional liars out of your children by affirming or pampering their weaknesses.

POOR THING, WHERE DOES IT HURT?

For your children's own good, teach them to maintain control of their emotions. If you do not want to produce sissies who use adversity as a chance to get attention, then don't program them that way. When your toddler falls over on the floor, don't run and pick him up, speaking in an alarmed, sympathetic voice.

I remember when I was only about eight years old, my cousin performed a stunt for the entertainment of all the adults present. His younger brother was sitting on the floor playing happily when my cousin said, "Watch this." Speaking to the infant in a pitiful, compassionate voice, he said, "Oh! Is the baby hurt? Poooorrr thiiinggg. What did you do? Does it hurt? Show it to Maaamaaaa." Sure enough, my cousin's happy little brother puckered up, started crying, and made his way to his mother for emotional support. To the roar of the adults, she picked him up, told him it would be all right, brushed off the imaginary dirt, and sat him back on the floor to continue happily playing. I was embarrassed for the little fellow, and wondered at the wisdom of the entertainment. An alarm went off in my head, and I suddenly had insight as to how my older, goofy cousins got to be the way they were. I tucked that thought away for future reference. Over the years I have observed that same phenomenon many times. Only once or twice was it done deliberately for entertainment. The other times it happened when a mother was rushing to her child's real or imagined distresses. The only one enjoying it was the super-sympathetic mother.

TOUGH TEENS

When I was just a young father, I had already determined that I would rear no sissies. If an infant fell and bumped his head in a manner that would not cause injury, we pretended to ignore it. In the event one of our toddlers took a spill, we let him lie, whimper a second, and then climb back up for another try. Sometimes a toddler would fall out of the wagon or stumble into the dirt; if there was no obvious harm done we let him deal with it. When the young ones wrecked their bicycles and skinned their knees, we paid no attention except to say something like, "You shouldn't go so fast until you learn to ride better." They would come in to dinner and we would see bloody knees or skinned hands and cheerfully ask, "What happened to you, Tiger?" "Oh, nothing. Just slid out on the curve in the loose gravel. I think I can make it next time." "Take it easy. You don't want to break something," we would respond.

Now our responses, or lack thereof, were not out of unconcern for our children's safety—quite the contrary. There were times when we had to hold each other back in order for our child to learn the lessons of life. The times when medical attention was necessary, we administered it calmly and efficiently, but returned them to their play to reassess what had gone wrong. We never had a child break a bone.

Your response to the actions and behavior of your children is important to the development of their character. You do not want to produce a teenager, and ultimately an adult, who hurts himself when he *needs* attention.

While still a youth, I saw a teenage girl who was jilted by a boyfriend feign being hurt. I also know an adult who hurts herself every time she gets emotionally disturbed. If, in your family, these extremes never occur, be grateful. It is far more pleasant to live with a child or teenager who is not a crybaby. Also, your daughter's future husband will appreciate you having trained her. And your sons will be far better men.

HOLD STILL

When our first daughter was a young girl, maybe seven or eight, I looked up to see a brown recluse spider crawling along her neck. Their bite is very cruel indeed. A pound of flesh may rot out where one bites. My daughter had been thoroughly taught to trust and obey us implicitly. I hastily commanded, "Don't move." She froze. Not a muscle twitched. Fear paled her eyes as she followed our intense stare and felt the creature creeping up her neck. I could see the rising compulsion to slap at it, to flee screaming. She stood perfectly rigid as I slowly approached, reached out, and carefully flicked the spider away. It was a wonderful sense of gratitude we shared for having trained her to maintain control of her emotions and trust us.

THE TUMBLING TOT

I was driving my truck some distance behind a horse-drawn hay-wagon when a little fellow about four or five years old fell off the back of the wagon onto the gravel road. No one had noticed him, and the wagon continued to rattle along. I started to go to his rescue, but he jumped up and ran to catch the wagon. After a couple of failed attempts to jump on, someone saw him and, grabbing a hand, swung him back into the wagon. After being seated, he rubbed his sore spots and continued on to the field. He did not expect the world to stop simply because he was lying in the road skinned up. I can imagine the fuss if that had happened to a modern, over-indulged child.

CRYING BABIES, OR CRYBABIES

When crawlers or "scooters" cry, there should be a legitimate reason. If they are hungry, feed them. If they are sleepy, put them down for a nap. If they are truly hurt, administer medical aid. If they are physically uncomfortable, adjust their environment. If they are wet, change them. If they are afraid, hold them close. If they are grouchy, discipline them to get control of their self-centeredness. If they are mad, switch them. Whatever the cause, don't let your child stay unhappy. Meet their *real needs* and make their selfish crying an unrewarding experience. The mother, especially, should be careful to anticipate the infant's needs and take care of them at appropriate times and levels. However, **when the infant is allowed to gain control of his environment through whining, *he* is training her.**

CHAPTER 18

Training in Self-Indulgence

HIS WIFE, SHE ATE NO LEAN

Early habits are lifelong habits. Why is it that some fat people find themselves compelled to eat when they become emotionally disturbed? When they get angry or depressed they go to the refrigerator as a way of coping. I have been told by grotesquely obese women that they wouldn't be fat if it were not for their compulsion to bury their disappointment under a stuffed belly.

Now obviously I am not attempting to define the cause of all fatness, or even the sole cause of some; but it is a contributing factor in many cases. How did this connection occur? The human/animal tendency to accept conditioning is extraordinary. Every time I think of an orange and imagine eating it, I have a muscular reaction in my jaw muscles. You probably had the same just reading that last sentence. I can experience sourness when the orange is still on the tree in Florida. Through repeated experiences I have been conditioned that way. It is involuntary. I cannot help the programmed response.

When a baby is breastfed, there are physical limitations to how often and when he can nurse. With a bottle-fed baby—even when the bottle is given after a year of breastfeeding—the bottle becomes a mighty convenient babysitter. An emotionally disturbed child can be quieted by simply poking a synthetic nipple into his mouth. As the food goes in, the tension and anxiety go out. An angry child can be pacified by a pacifier or bottle. A child can be put to sleep with food. You can purchase for yourself a reprieve from almost anything through a bottle or pacifier. But what are you doing to your child?

Not only is he failing to learn self-control, HE IS LEARNING TO COPE BY PUTTING SOMETHING IN HIS MOUTH.

The addiction to cigarettes is not all nicotine. Have you ever noticed how a person who quits smoking will often keep something in his mouth? Many a tree has been eaten one matchstick or toothpick at a time by former smokers attempting to pacify their addiction to sucking on something.

Many fat people have little desire for food early in the day. Not until the day's responsibilities mount up do they begin to nurse their insecurities. Late at night, when the problems of the day have accumulated and are left unresolved, the refrigerator becomes their emotional support.

I am convinced that parents who provide overly extended emotional consolation through food or the sucking sensation are training their children to be self-gratifying and self-indulgent. *Temperance* is part of the fruit of the Spirit (Gal. 5:23) that should be evident in all of us. Parent, if you not only cater to your child's appetite but actually employ it as a means of purchasing compliance, what are you instilling? Remember, the first human sin involved eating. The Devil's first temptation to the Son of God involved eating. *"And put a knife to thy throat, if thou be a man given to appetite"* (Prov. 23:2). There is a spiritual principle involved here that goes far deeper. **To allow lack of self-control in any area of life is to condition the child to be generally intemperate.**

INHERITED INTEMPERANCE

Intemperance is passed on from parent to child. A parent's example of intemperance in one area may be manifested in the child by a lack of self-control in another area. Some older children so despise their parents' weakness that they take special care to not fall victim. Yet the parental example of intemperance will manifest itself in another area of the child's life where their guard is not up. Parents who are intemperate regarding food may have skinny children who become intemperate in their use of drugs. Parents who are intemperate with possessions may have children who are intemperate in the way they spend money. Intemperance in any area is a grave, destructive sin, like a cancer that metastasizes to other parts of the body. Your children will reap what you sow. *"Be not deceived; God is not mocked: for whatsoever a man soweth, that shall he also reap. For he that soweth to his flesh shall of the flesh reap corruption . . ."* (Gal. 6:7–8). *"Man shall not live by bread alone . . ."* (Matt. 4:4).

If you, as an adult, realize that your parents passed on their intemperance to you, you can either blame them and continue letting your belly be your god (Phil. 3:19) or you can throw off the curse rather than pass it on to your children.

I have sadly observed many children being trained in the art of selfish indulgence by their parents' readiness to shower them with tinsel and fluff. A child raised with commercial gadgets heaped upon his lusts is much more prone to be envious and covetous than the poor child who finds satisfaction in the simple things of life. The child who grows up deprived of nothing is greatly handicapped in real life. Never consider your affluence to be an advantage to your children. It is a handicap for which you must compensate. Examine carefully and prayerfully Jesus's words regarding the disadvantages of the rich (Mark 4:19; Luke 12:15; 1 Tim. 6:6–19; James 5:1–5).

CHAPTER 19

Bullies

IS EVERYONE HAVING FUN?

One of the rules—more of a principle-—in our home is: "If it is not fun for all, it is not fun at all." Where there is more than one child, good, honest sparring sometimes degenerates into bullying. We stayed out of their personal conflict as much as possible, standing back and letting them work through it. A pecking order is inevitable, but if it got out of hand or they came to us with sincere concerns, then we would step in to arbitrate.

BLOWING UP

Let's create a likely scenario: One of the girls is trying to blow up a balloon while the brother, several years older, is preventing her from accomplishing her task and laughing at her helpless protests. It starts out with her involved in the game, but she soon tires and starts to earnestly resist. He is having such fun that he continues with increased vigor to thwart her efforts. She is getting aggravated and is now complaining. He laughs louder. She starts physically resisting, jerking away, swinging her elbows, and yelling, "Stop it!" He doggedly pursues his goal of proving his prowess as chief balloon-deflator. Daddy steps in: "Okay, what's the problem?" "Oh, nothing. We're just playing," the brother says. She protests, "He won't let me blow up my balloon." It is time now for a little training and reproof.

The wrong way to handle this would be to impatiently yell, "Give her the balloon so she will shut up. And get out of here; I can't hear myself think!" The brother would toss it over with an "I beat you" sneer, and she would try to blow it up in his presence to prove her victory. They would continue to silently compete until another opportunity for mischief arose. This would happen between them as many as thirty times a day. You might try switching each of them two or three times, to no effect. She would become a whining tattletale, and he would become a sulking bully. You are functioning like a referee who came expecting a fight, and you are there to keep it fair. Instead, you should be functioning as a teacher of righteousness.

Try this approach. Calmly say, "What's going on here?" The brother responds, "Oh, nothing. We're just playing." Daddy says, "Sister, are you having fun?" She says, "No, he won't let me blow up my balloon." Daddy says to the boy, "Are you having fun?" He looks abashed and says, "Well, we were just playing." Daddy asks, "Brother, was sister having fun?" "No, I guess not." "Could you tell that she wasn't having fun?" "Well, I guess so." "What do you mean, you guess so? Did you or did you not think she was having fun?" "Well, I knew she wasn't having fun." "Were you having fun when your sister was suffering?" Silence. "Can you have fun by making someone else unhappy?" Silence. He looks at the floor. "Look at me. How would you like it if someone bigger than you treated you like that?" "I wouldn't," he answers. Then I would say my famous lines, "If everyone is not having fun, then it is not fun at all. Son, you know Hitler and his men had fun when others were suffering. They laughed while boys and girls cried in pain. Do you want to grow up to be like Hitler?" In complete brokenness, he says, "No, Daddy, I don't want to be like Hitler. I didn't mean to make her unhappy. Sister, I am sorry." What great training! The brother and sister will go away bonded and sympathetic. The sister forgives because she has seen his repentance and feels sorry for his grief. She is drawn to him. He will be more protective of her. They both have been restored.

Your reproof will produce repentance only if the boy sees genuineness and fairness in you. If he detects in you any lack of the benevolence you advocate, he will not repent. He will just become hard and bitter.

If he has ever taken offense at the way you have talked to his mother, he will not experience repentance until he sees you express the same. If the boy does not show repentance after it is clear he understands the issues, a spanking would be in order, followed by further reproof and reasoning. If there is still no repentance ensuing in forgiveness and love to his sister, then it becomes clear he has a deeper, more long-term problem, one that requires rebuilding of relationships and careful management.

CHAPTER 20

"Religious" Whips

HATERS OF GOD

I have cringed at seeing parents use God to intimidate their children into obedience. A child has been "bad," and the mother warns, "You shouldn't do that; God doesn't like it." Or worse, "God is going to get you for that." And again, "Mama might not see it, but God does." Talk about negative, counterproductive training! If you constrain a child by threatening him with divine displeasure, he will come to hate God and will throw off religion as soon as he is old enough for independent action. It happens with regularity. Never, I say, **NEVER use God to threaten or intimidate your child into compliance.** You are causing the child to associate God with condemnation and rejection. You should teach your children of God's judgments, of heaven and hell, and the awful consequences of sin, but not as a means to manipulate their daily behavior.

When I was a young teenager at summer camp, there were several boys who got rowdy late at night. The angry directors disciplined them by making them sit and read the Bible. One night at about 2 a.m., I got up to use the bathroom and saw them sitting there with open Bibles in their laps, wearing surly expressions. At that young age, yet loving the Scripture myself, and while knowing nothing of psychology, I distinctly remember being grieved for what I knew was going to be the result of this "discipline." The staff was conditioning these young men to hate the Bible. With a burning resentment in their hearts, every time they looked down at its pages they were associating the Bible with their bitter spirit. Three or four hours of this could leave an aversion for Scripture that, with further reinforcement, could continue throughout the rest of their lives. It would have been far better if one of the directors had worked with the boys mopping floors. Then he could have bonded with them and had opportunity to instruct them in a non-condemning way.

I know a mother who makes her children look up Bible verses for punishment. The exercise itself could be good training, except when it occurs as a way of dealing with rebellion. The rebellion should be resolved by the rod and reproof.

GOOD MEMORIES ARE WELCOMED

Don't use your devotional time as a clearinghouse for settling grievances. Family worship should never be a time to "call someone on the carpet." No one has good feelings about being called to the principal's office. The school principal did the really serious paddling when I was a young student, and he and I had a couple of those stern encounters. I have lived nearly a half century and still feel apprehension when going into the office at a public school. One of these days I might just make an effigy of a school principal and then tell him to bend over and grab his ankles.

On the other hand, when I see pastel drawing chalk, I remember old Mrs. Johnson, my art teacher, smiling and setting up a still life for us to draw. I would go back there and spend hours, if I could.

What memories and associations are you filing away in your child's subconscious, lifelong memory banks? Teach the Bible in your home. Give them exercises of looking up verses on patience, love, faithfulness, and so forth, but don't do it as a response to their failure in some area. If they should have weaknesses that demand instruction, wait until the pressure and condemnation are off before giving them a study in those areas. If there are guilt feelings present, the lesson will only bring further condemnation and isolation that the rod cannot absolve. When the instruction about God is separate from your discipline, they are free to make an application or association without feeling watched and graded. Otherwise you will end up with children working for God's approval—as well as yours—instead of enjoying the peace of God which passes all understanding. Allow the Spirit of God to apply truths to your child's consciousness at his level. An adult's sense of discernment is more highly developed. Don't cause them to have a foreboding of God before they are mature enough to see everything in perspective.

CHAPTER 21

Imitations

CHRISTIAN PARENTS' PARROTS

One way to dull your children's sensitivity to God is to make them religious show-offs. Parents who value the outward displays of devotion fall into the "Pharisee syndrome." Don't train your children in the skills of religious pretense. Don't train them to be *as the hypocrites are: for they love to pray standing in the synagogues and in the corners of the streets, that they may be seen of men. Verily I say unto you, they have their reward"* (Matt. 6:5).

The other day I invited my family out to see our dog do a new trick. I gave the command, but he was too distracted by them to regard me. I had interrupted their schedule with the promise of a trick, and the dog acted as if he had never seen me before, much less knew what I was commanding. I became anxious and started pushing him to perform. He was making me look silly. "What right does he have to do this to me? Me, of all people? My family would have thought I was so smart, and now I look so dumb. Stupid dog! Must be inbred." Sensing my disapproval, he started to shy away from me. To get my approval, he must make me look good in public. After all, what is a dog good for but to elevate his master? Right?

I have had parents bring their little child in, stand him in front of me, and say, "Say, 'praise the Lord' for Brother Mike." When he has finished his performance, everyone smiles and praises him. The parents grin as if they just heard the announcement that their dog had won the annual Frisbee-catching contest. When little children are cute in their prayers or religious imitations, they should be totally ignored. Otherwise, you encourage hypocrisy and pride. Never teach them to act out a *"form of godliness"* instead of living it by the power of the Spirit (2 Tim. 3:5). **It is a cheap trick to school your children to appear ahead of their peers in religious devotions.** You and your children will only be rewarded here and now, and that is all the reward such stage playing ever gets. *"Verily I say unto you, they have their reward"* (Matt. 6:5).

One well-meaning father has two children who sing fairly well. Every chance he gets, he captures an audience to listen to their singing. Their gospel songs, sung by another, would be a blessing; but when sung in exhibition as a way of showing off, it is a pain to endure. "Their singing is so cute." As they parade back to their seats, he praises them, smiling as I would have if my dog had performed when I wanted him to.

One time when the two singing parrots forgot the words and showed a little indifference to performing, the audience became restless and the father became anxious. His act was falling apart. He coaxed and encouraged until I saw in him the same feelings I had toward my non-performing dog. Now, the dog is obviously not going to suffer from being "paraded," but these children are already suffering. The father's ambition for himself and his children overrides his concern for their spiritual well-being. Or maybe he doesn't have the wisdom to discern the difference. It is easy to come to ruin in this body of pride and lust, as Solomon so aptly warns us: *"Pride goeth before destruction, and an haughty spirit before a fall"* (Prov. 16:18).

We are all subject to the weaknesses of the flesh and will at some point do or say something stupid. Stupid is human, but that doesn't change the fact that stupid is ugly. The higher road is to admit stupid from time to time and keep truckin'.

CHAPTER 22

Homeschool Makes No Fools

THE SYSTEM

One judge in Nebraska said that the public educational system is preparing the children of America for a merger into the New World Order. He went on to say that the children of Christian homeschool families would not fit into the planned system.

Never even consider sending your teen children to private Christian schools, much less the public automaton factories. Whether a classroom is based completely on Christian education or on secular principles is not the issue. **God didn't make teenage boys and girls to sit together in a classroom every day while real life outside passes them by.** The world's system digs a pit and then creates a myriad of industries to reclaim the tragic lives that fall into it. Classroom education for the young is a moral pit. The psychiatrists, counselors, social workers, Planned Parenthood, policemen, social planners, juvenile courts, drug dealers, penal institutions, pharmaceutical companies, and medical doctors all stand at the edge of the pit competing for the business generated by the shovels of the National Education Association.

One important warning: There exists a fundamental fault that is demonstrated in the discouragement experienced by many homeschool families. Because the public educational system is based on false premises, its curriculum, its format, and its purpose are all in error. The homeschool is not established to duplicate the public school and its curriculum in a private environment. Yet most homeschoolers are attempting to do that very thing. The stress on the family attempting to perform for the sake of public image as well as state-required testing is destructive to the emotional and intellectual development of the child.

Ask yourself this question: "If I did not have to answer to anyone, and I were not controlled by public opinion, what would I desire for my children to learn in their early years of education?" Keep in mind that specialty disciplines necessary for professional employment need not be taught by either the classroom or the homeschool. Those things can be learned when the child is emotionally mature and ready to enter the workplace.

Parents, you are wearing yourselves out trying to keep up with the judges. Teach from your heart, not from the John Dewey perspective. **Children need a mother who teaches them, not a teacher who doesn't have the emotional energy to mother them. Young men need a father who teaches them to work, not a father too busy working to teach them.**

The best schooling for children is a good home life, not a home that is all school. It is a sick perversion to remove a child from that which is natural to life and make of him a professional student. **Don't accept the false premise that academic and behavioral education is the foundation of life and society.** Order your own life according to God's perspective. Your children are too valuable for you to compromise their training.

If you fear your children are too isolated from the world and need what the progressives call *socialization,* then get yourself a TV and sit them down in front of Hollywood for about two hours every day. They will soon be duplicates of the public school, frequenters of the local hangouts, and accepting of back-alley morality. Put your children to the breast of Hollywood, and they will never desire to be nurtured on the *"milk of the word."* Hollywood is a far more effective teacher than you will ever be, sponsored by none other than the prince of the power of the air (waves). And Hollywood has an aggressive, appealing agenda acceptable to most of modern-day society.

If you want a child who will easily integrate into the New World Order, waiting his turn in line for condoms, a government-funded abortion, sexually transmitted disease treatment, psychological evaluation, and a mark on the forehead, then follow the popular guidelines in today's education, entertainment, and social norms. But if you want a son or daughter of God, you will have to do it God's way and in God's choice of location—the home.

Update (2015): I have wanted to leave this book as originally published, but the foregoing section speaking of the evils of the TV is so out of date, I must address more recent trends in technology. What seemed like great temptation for children 21 years ago now seems like *Little House on the Prairie*.

Last Sunday as I was speaking in church, I noticed three boys, just past the age of puberty, sitting together on the very back row. They were passing a cell phone around, laughing at what they were viewing on the screen. That couldn't have happened 21 years ago. At that time a child had to discover a *Playboy* magazine hidden in his father's garage to view naked women. Today, every child with a cell phone can view hardcore pornography that would have landed a man in jail two decades ago. We have seen the last generation before descent into total Sodom. When parents cannot take their thirteen-year-old boys to a home church of about fifty people and know they will be safe from the evils of Bangkok, Thailand, what is left?

> 3 *If the **foundations be destroyed,** what can the righteous do?*
>
> 4 *The LORD is in his holy temple, the LORD'S throne is in heaven: his eyes behold, his eyelids try, the children of men.*
>
> 5 *The LORD trieth the righteous: but the wicked and him that loveth violence his soul hateth.*
>
> 6 *Upon the wicked he shall rain snares, fire and brimstone, and an horrible tempest: this shall be the portion of their cup.*
>
> 7 *For the righteous LORD loveth righteousness; his countenance doth behold the upright.* (Psalm 11:3–7)

When you consider texting, sexting, Facebook, Twitter, Snapchat, and the social media that will supplant these, we know there is no place for part-time parenting or naïvety.

> *For the LORD knoweth the way of the righteous: but the way of the ungodly shall perish.* (Psalm 1:6)

CHAPTER 23

The Flavor of Joy

This chapter is an adaptation of an article written by Michael Pearl and first published in No Greater Joy *magazine, May 1995.*

Parenting, like courtship, must be properly seasoned with joy. Parenting without joy is not only tasteless, it is tiresome, even unpleasant. Joy is the only foundation on which meaningful relationships can be built. Parenting without joy is like music without rhythm, or flowers without color. A joyless parent can no more raise happy kids than can a skunk raise skunklets that smell good. You say, "But the kids destroy my joy!" What? How can that be when the kids would say that you are destroying their joy? If someone were to ask your children if you were joyful, what would they say?

REASONS FOR LACK OF JOY

Most often, joylessness is caused by a failure to properly train the children. If you are not proactive with well-thought-out child-training techniques, the whole family will be so confused and confrontational that a joyful person in your family would look like the court fool.

In many homes, the problems are not deep—bad, yes, but not deep. Sometimes, especially in large families, there is no deep-seated hostility or resentment, just chaos, like at an intersection with no traffic light. The problem there is lack of organization and management. Parents fail to train and don't respond to the needs of the children until they are provoked into responding to the ensuing intolerable behavior. Then they are only reacting and doing damage control, not training.

Their home is like a city with few traffic lights, directional signals, or road signs. Everybody is trying to survive in a lawless atmosphere. Parents must install traffic lights and road signs and consistently enforce the laws if they are going to stop the collisions. Once everyone knows the rules and parents assume the role of manager and overseer, order is reestablished, tension melts away, and everyone is joyful with the new order.

When parents don't organize, they end up spending most of their time expressing their displeasure at the way everything is going. Their negative attitudes create distance between themselves and their children—a spirit of antagonism. The children take a cue from their parents and fight among themselves. It creates an environment with too many problems to address. Joy is not possible in an atmosphere where no one is satisfied with anyone or anything.

With only a little enlightenment, many parents have applied these simple training procedures and gained complete control of their families in just a few days. By assuming their God-ordained authority with dignity and joy, these parents have eliminated the provocation to anger in their children, as well as in themselves. Their anger was a product of their frustration. Theirs was just a runaway condition that was begging to be halted. The establishment of consistent authority in the home was welcomed and it made everyone happy. Joy and color and music came back to the family.

THE OTHER REASON FOR LACK OF JOY

Careful organization with consistent enforcement will put an end to 90% of the conflict. When everyone is functioning as part of the family society, there is little provocation to anger, but parenting doesn't stop with conditioning children to outward obedience. It is a blessing to have the circumstantial anger removed, to have peace in the home; but the absence of conflict does not necessarily imply joy. **Joy is a positive virtue, not just the absence of conflict.**

In contrast to joylessness caused by outward confusion, some parents are joyless within their own souls—regardless of the circumstances. They may not be angry or unhappy, just joyless. Look at it as a balance scale. Anger or bitterness is on the far left; a stable, sedate personality is in the middle; and joyfulness is on the far right. Granted, children do far better with deadpan parents who have neither joy nor anger than they do with angry or bitter parents, but they do best when both parents are known for their joy. Bitterness is a plant with a disease. Joyless mediocrity is a plant without disease growing in average-to-poor soil. Joyfulness is a plant rooted in well-balanced soil with the right combination of rain and sunshine.

The Bible tells us to bring up our children in the nurture and admonition of the Lord. It is an oxymoron to claim to be nurturing without joy. You may train the outside of a young child with proper technique, but the child's soul can only be nurtured and trained with joy. I have said on many occasions, "If the joy of the Lord is the Christian's strength, is not the joy of the parent the child's strength?"

ROLE MODELS

Children must be attracted to their parents by something more than physical lineage. Parents are competing with many others in an open contest for the position of role model. Children will seek to be like the person who is most attractive to them. Parents cannot demand respect or admiration. If it is not freely given, it doesn't exist. Joy attracts everyone. Small children can be molded by proper application of good technique and good psychology, but older children can see right through insincerity and hypocrisy. You must be real to win the approval of a teenager.

Children are rooted in parental attitudes more than in proper technique. More parenting is caught than taught. As salt that has lost its savor is good for nothing but to be cast out and trampled underfoot, so parenting that has lost its joy results in a family that will be trampled underfoot. Just as parenting without training is chaos, training without joy is tyranny.

If there is no joy, what is the point? A soldier can endure the mud, blood, and pain of war by fantasizing of past or future joys, but a child reared without joy is a lost soul. A man can endure a workplace that affords no joy because he knows that there is a sanctuary of joy waiting for him at home. But when the sanctuary is joyless, what hope can sustain him? A mature wife may even cope with a joyless marriage by consoling herself in the hope of the afterlife, but a child cannot so resign himself. A husband may deal with a joyless marriage by losing himself in the rewards of work or hobbies, but a child has no outlet that can compensate for loss of joyful relationships. Relationships are a very important part of the adult world, but friendly, joyful relationships are all the world to a child—his only reality. An adult without relationships may still be a successful careerist, leader, or hobbyist, but a child without happy relationships will be emotionally ill, in desperate need of help. Where there is no joy you have nothing to offer anyone.

The archenemy of joy is bitterness. If Christ were joy, Antichrist would be bitterness. No matter the skill or technique, as a painting created by a bitter artist expresses bitterness on the canvas, so parenting done in bitterness will leave its marks on the canvas of the child's soul. Bitterness is like a virus; it multiplies until it infects all healthy tissue. It is rottenness to the bones. It doesn't matter if a parent's unhappiness is not related to the child; a parent's unhappiness affects the child all the same.

PLANTED IN JOY

Creativity is conceived in the womb of joy and is almost nonexistent in a depressed or critical atmosphere. God created humans to be happy. Happiness and joy are a healing balm. Children who rise up a little grumpy and meet a smiling mother are soon smiling with her. On the other hand, children who rise up grumpy and meet a grump will only spiral downward into bickering and whining. Parents think, "I am tired of them being grouchy; I will put pressure on them until they straighten up." But pressure never causes a sapling to grow straight.

A little girl who gets up with a chip on her shoulder should meet a smiling mother who is undaunted by her cloudy expression and greets her with exclamations of delight. If the child is not soon infused with joy, she certainly should never be allowed to alter the mood of the family. She should be treated as the offending one; she has cut herself out of the fun with her bad attitude. If a grumpy child can change the atmosphere of the home to reflect her bad mood, then in her estimation she is justified in her grouchiness.

You cannot threaten, insult, or intimidate a bad attitude out of a child. If you respond in anger, the child cannot help but view your discipline as a personal confrontation. It is perfectly natural then for the child to reciprocate by further reacting in anger.

WHAT IS THE SOURCE?

Finally, ask yourself this question: Is my lack of joy a result of my circumstances alone? If you took the proper steps to organize and manage your home, and in so doing trained your children to be a decent and orderly part of it, would you then be joyful? Or does your lack of joy result from something *within yourself,* or maybe something that is *not in you?* If it is all circumstantial then you should be able to reverse the trend in just a few days of training. Many testify that their first day of training transforms everyone, in which case the problem was shallow, just procedural. Their technique was off, and so proper training immediately restored the joy. They were unhappy from circumstances without, not from unhappiness within.

But if you are unhappy from within, then applying proper training techniques will help some, but it will not bring the children to where they should be, and it will certainly not give you lasting joy. If your unhappiness is in your soul, then you must go to a soul doctor. Jesus Christ is the only licensed soul doctor in the universe. All others are fakes. John the apostle said, *"And these things write we unto you, that your **joy** may be full"* (1 John 1:4).

Perhaps you need to confess your sinfulness to God and pray with David, *"Restore unto me the **joy** of thy salvation"* (Psalm 51:12). And as Nehemiah said to the people when they were overcome with grief over their sin, *"Neither be ye sorry; for the **joy** of the LORD is your strength"* (Neh. 8:10). Then David rejoiced in God's forgiveness, saying, *"And my soul shall be **joyful** in the LORD"* (Psalm 35:9).

Paul sums up the entire Christian experience, saying, *"For the kingdom of God is not meat and drink; but righteousness, and peace, and **joy** in the Holy Ghost"* (Rom. 14:17). **Religion without joy is God-less.**

Finally, here is the Scripture upon which we based our magazine: *"I have no greater joy than to hear that my children walk in truth"* (3 John 4). There is truly *No Greater Joy* on earth than the flavor of joy that emanates from the happy, joyful family. May it be true for all of us. God bless each of you as you train up your children for Him—with great joy.

CHAPTER 24

Personal

It has been twenty-one years since the first edition of this book. I was forty-eight years old at the first publication. My older son was seventeen, and my younger son was fifteen. I am now sixty-nine years old with twenty-two grandchildren and two more on the way. My children are in their thirties and early forties. All five of them bring joy to our hearts. I must risk sounding like a braggart. Or maybe I should say I cannot help but brag; we have not been disappointed by any of our children. They have exceeded our expectations. They are the best of people, and they continue to bring us great joy. Some of the grandkids are teenagers. Unbelievable! How time flies when you're having fun!

Twenty-one years ago I wrote an admonition to my two sons, and Deb wrote to our three daughters. We have retained those admonitions as originally written.

LETTER TO MY SONS, 1994

There is always the possibility that I could be gone by the time they have children of their own. When I think about them getting married and rearing children, there is so much I would like to see them keep in mind. So in summary, I will address a letter to my two sons.

Gabriel and Nathan Pearl,

I cannot imagine the kind of world tomorrow will bring, but unless it is the Millennium spoken of in the Bible, it will be even more hostile to the family. If the Lord should tarry long enough for you to marry and begin rearing children, your dad has a few words of advice.

First, know that the woman you marry will be the lifelong mother of your children. All that she is in the accumulation of her past experiences will be present as the mother of your children. There is not a more major decision affecting the future of your children than the choice of your life's partner. The relationship between a man and his wife has more influence on their children than any other factor. While a couple may carefully express their differences only in private, they cannot hide the effects from their children. Remember, sons, your family will be no better than the relationship you have with your wife—their mother.

Be sure to cultivate your relationship with your wife. Meet her needs. Make her happy. *Enjoy her thoroughly.* Her state of mind is going to be 50% of your children's example, 100% when you are not there. If you will love and cherish your wife, the children will love and cherish her also. If you are a servant to her, your example will translate to their experience.

When you look for a wife and mother for your children, the first qualification is that she **love the Lord** and be his true disciple. Nothing else will adequately equip her for the duration. She will need to know how to pray. A girl who takes Christ for granted will do the same with her family. A man and his wife are *"heirs together of the grace of life"* (1 Pet. 3:7). It takes two, equally yoked, to pull the family wagon safely through the hostile deserts and minefields of this "last days" society we have inherited.

The second thing to look for in a prospective wife is **cheerfulness.** While some might ignore this qualification altogether, I can't emphasize too forcefully the value and practicality of this quality. A girl who is unhappy and discontent before marriage will NOT suddenly change afterwards. Every prospective wife out there has already experienced trials and adversities in her short life, as have you. The happy, cheerful girl has learned to deal with them, and *still* enjoys life. No man can make a discontented woman happy. A woman who does not find joy from a wellspring within will not find it in the difficulties and trials of marriage and motherhood.

Courtship is a garden in spring—everybody's garden looks promising then. But *marriage* is a garden in August, when the quality of the soil and seed and all the care to guard against pestilence, blight, and weeds begin to manifest themselves. The fruit of the womb can be spoiled before germination. Give special, prayerful care to the choice of a wife and mother. A girl who easily and often gets her feelings hurt and cries in order to manipulate you will be a ball and chain after you are married. Look for that cheerfulness when things are not exactly the way she likes them.

The next quality to look for is **thankfulness.** When a young girl is unthankful toward her family or her circumstances, a change of environment and relationships is not going to make her thankful. Thankfulness is not so much a response to one's environment as it is an expression of the heart. Avoid a moody, unthankful, unhappy girl. If she is not full of the joy of living before marriage, she surely will not be afterwards. A young lady who had been married less than a month said to your mom, "I have never in my life been one to have my feelings hurt. But since I got married, I seem to go around with a chip on my shoulder. I guess it is just that I care more than I once did." Your mother corrected her, "No, you don't care more; you just feel that you have more rights now, and therefore you are *expecting* more." The thing to remember is that personalities and temperaments do not improve after marriage. When the social restraints are lifted, the freedom that comes only from a secure union permits one to express true feelings.

Boys, take note of a girl's attitude toward her father. It doesn't matter what kind of louse he may be; if she is rebellious to him, she will be twice as rebellious to you. If she speaks disrespectfully of him or to him, she will do likewise to you.

Another thing to look for is a creative, hard worker. Don't marry a lazy, slothful girl. Beauty can get mighty old lying up in bed, framed in a disheveled, griping, slothful pout. Whatever you do, avoid a lazy girl. If she expects to be waited on, let her marry a waiter. You will have a full job rearing the children without having to rear a wife.

Never marry a girl who feels she is not getting the best man in the world when she gets you. A girl who enters marriage thinking she could have done better will never be satisfied for wondering what it might have been like if . . .

Avoid the girl who is enamored with her own looks. Better to marry a homely girl who is content to love and be loved than one who is going to spend her years trying to maintain her fading beauty. Life is too big and full to be spent waiting on a disappointed woman who is regretfully looking in the mirror. Let her be one who lets you be the judge of her beauty, and remind her often of it. After all, it was that beauty in her that attracted you to her in the first place.

Avoid like the plague the girl who will pursue her own career outside the home. A wife must be your "help meet."

The last qualification is a **love for children.** A girl who doesn't want her life encumbered with children is suffering a deep hurt and is walking a road to misery. One day, the Lord willing, you are going to have children of your own. They must have a mother who loves and delights in them.

Now, I want to speak to you about being good fathers. While you are still young and unmarried, with no children, do what all of God's creatures do—prepare the nest for their arrival. DON'T PUT YOURSELF IN AN OCCUPATIONAL POSITION THAT WILL LEAVE YOU *OUT OF POSITION* TO BE A GOOD FATHER. Plan your life's trade so as to maximize your role as father. Fathers who become absorbed in their success in business will make lousy fathers. If you gain the whole world and lose your child's soul, what profit is it? Some workaholics will say they are doing it for their children—providing security, a good education, etc. Why is it that the children of hard-working, absent fathers never appreciate their sacrifice, and even show disdain and contempt for their father's success? The reason is that children are not fooled. They understand their father's absence to be selfishness on his part and lack of interest in them. They see their father getting more satisfaction from his job than from their presence. Whether this be true or not, the results are the same. Business success always passes away; time spent with your children becomes a permanent, eternal part of them. The education your child will need cannot be purchased at a university. It is purchased by the father in the many hours spent doing things with his children.

The modern concept of *quality* time as opposed to *quantity* is a salve for the consciences of progressive parents thoroughly wrapped up in worldly pursuits. A scheduled hour of clinical-like attention makes your "quality time" nothing more than the fulfillment of a business appointment—a therapy session. It can be unreal and pretentious. Insincere attention to inconsequential matters cheapens real fellowship with your children. Your best time together will be that which is spent in real struggles to achieve common goals. A child will build self-worth, not by being the center of attention in idle chatter, but by actually conquering a real-world need—putting up a mailbox, a clothesline, cutting the grass, bringing in firewood, washing windows, building a doghouse, or going on the father's job and being a real helper.

Do you remember when Don Madill would come to work in our cabinet shop with his little two- or three-year-old son hanging around, cleaning up sawdust or hammering a nail? There was no pretense or haste in that father-son relationship. Today, his sons are little "men," secure in their role.

As soon as your first child is born, begin your role as father. Relieve your tired wife for a couple of hours a day by taking the infant and attending to all his needs. When you are reading or resting, lay the child on your lap. When you boys were only a few days old, I would lay you on my chest to sleep out a restless night. I got to where I could sleep soundly with you like a little puddle on top of me. Your exhausted mother needed a break.

When I was newly married, I expected my wife to be a "super" woman. I soon learned that if she were going to last through several more childbirths—and that in good spirits—she was going to need a lot of support. Treat your wife as a delicate flower, and she will "bloom" with energy to be a more giving mother.

I am aware that you boys don't need much sleep. However, if you experienced a major operation every two to three years, having a twenty-pound "tumor" removed, and you had to lend your body to a dairy farmer, you would need a little more rest too. Allow your wife to sleep a little longer than you do, and she will be more efficient.

Though I spent a lot of time with you when you were young, I always told your mother, "They are yours until they can follow me outside and then they are mine." Take your little ones along on many adventures. Explore and discover the world all over again with each one. I used to take you rabbit hunting in a backpack. My rabbit dogs got so conditioned that when they saw me with a backpack they just knew we were going hunting. I think Rebekah was glad when Gabriel came along and displaced her from the old rumble seat.

Provide lots of "junk" for your children to exercise their creativity with—cardboard boxes, wooden blocks, sawdust, sand, sticks, hammers, and nails. Avoid store-bought playthings that can stifle creativity by limiting imagination.

An important principle to remember is that the more time you spend doing things together, the fewer discipline problems you will have. A child who adores his father will want to please him in everything. **A child can't rebel against his best buddy.** When they are big enough to look at pictures in a book, spend time turning pages with them. When they are old enough to understand, begin reading or telling Bible stories. Throughout the day, as it is natural, tell them of our Heavenly Father. Together examine nature as the wise creation of a magnificent God.

Don't put off spending time being a daddy. Each day they grow without you is like a tomato plant growing without being staked. It spreads without direction, and weeds come up inside where they cannot be seen or easily removed. Without staking, the fruit will be brought forth on the ground, where it will rot.

A father who is *there,* always involved in his child's life, will know the heartbeat of his child. **If you will praise and reward the desired behavior, there will be very little undesirable behavior.** You will be speaking fifty encouraging words for every rebuke.

But don't fall prey to the modern psychological jargon that promotes running in to say something positive to bolster up a child you've neglected. It is artificial, and it is flattery. Positive statements that are not warranted by legitimate good works are destructive. **A child should know that he has earned every word of praise.** Praise not based on deserving works is as unjust as is punishment without provocation. It will teach a lie because it reverses reality. There is no substitute for real-life presence. If your child is not doing anything praiseworthy, then take his hand to walk beside you until he does do something worthy. Neglected children become rejected children. A child must have his father as a plant must have light to grow healthy. A flash-bulb approach is not sufficient. **A slow, steady shining of the father's presence is what is needed.**

Don't ever leave the spiritual training to their mother (no matter how good a job she does), otherwise the children will grow up thinking religion is for women. You put the children to bed in the evening and read and pray with them.

As your boys get older, make sure they are not confined to studies too much. By the time they are twelve or thirteen, they should be finished with structured school and be involved in an occupation with you. Continue to expose them to concepts and ideas; but, above all, provide real-life problems that they must solve—bicycle, small engine, or appliance repair. All forms of building and maintenance are essential training.

The concept you are seeking to convey is one of independence and confidence. A child who can do it, fix it, or make it will try new things and expect to succeed. The confidence learned in work will translate to success in education—and life itself.

Remember the twenty-seven-year-old Amish fellow with his first car, going off to college in a faraway city, leaving all the things that were familiar, facing challenges never before considered. I was apprehensive about his ability to succeed in this new environment. He had none of the necessary skills. His educational ability was about equal to that of a sixth-grader.

When I tried to warn him of the difficulties ahead, he said, "I have always been able to do everything I tried to do; I can do this also." It was hard on him, but he got a B average the first semester. Whether it was the product of his hands or his head, he had learned to succeed.

If you burden a young child with studies to the point of making him feel inadequate, you are building a foundation for failure in him. First, teach your children to work with their hands, and the education of their minds will come more readily. Don't leave your boys at home with mother and the girls in a classroom setting. They should be out with the men.

Boys, guide your wives to understand training and discipline. Don't take for granted that they are automatically equipped to be mothers. Some mothers don't have the courage to discipline. They will tell the children, "Just wait until your daddy gets home; he will spank you." When you walk through the door, you will want the kids to come climbing on your legs and pulling on your arms, not cowering in a corner. Three hours of dreading Daddy's coming home can be devastating programming. Train your wife to do her own discipline.

Check yourself for balance by asking the question: "Do my children view me as a stern and severe disciplinarian or as a cheerful and wonderful companion and guide?" **Your judgments and punishments should be lost in the many happy hours of communion with them.**

Lastly, as your children develop, let them feel a part of the struggles of life. Don't become so financially "successful" that you can provide everything they need or want. If you find that everything is coming too easily, be willing to give it all away and start over under more difficult circumstances.

Life without struggle is not achievement. If they lose their shoes, let them go without until they can make the money to buy more. Make sure you do not have all the delicacies available to eat. Let them learn to be content doing without.

Keep the sugar and junk food out of the house. If they never have it, they will not want it. If eating between meals prevents them from eating real food (meat, potatoes, vegetables, salads, etc.), then don't let them eat except at mealtime.

There are some flavors or textures that we all simply have an aversion for. Allow each child one or two dislikes; just don't let their preferences be too limited. Liking a lot of different foods is good, and not liking one or two certainly isn't going to hurt them. If a child doesn't like what is on the table, let him do without until the next meal. A little fasting is good training. If you have a child who is particularly finicky and only eats a limited diet, then feed him mainly what he doesn't like until he likes it.

Forget about buying them toys. Some functional toys are desirable, like a metal truck for the little boys, or a tricycle or bicycle for the older ones. Little girls can profit from play dishes and baby dolls (which resemble real babies). Just don't cultivate their covetous inclinations by teaching them to expect to have their lusts indulged.

Never yield to fads. Christians should have too much dignity to be carried along by the Madison Avenue promoters. Their shoes, clothes, and cereals should be chosen for serviceability, not style.

Hollywood is not for God's children. Don't allow the brainless, subversive, Sesame Street–type propaganda into your house. Your children's thinking should be molded by the Word of God and Christian example, not by sex perverts and socialists. If you want to destroy your family, then get yourself a good TV and DVD player to keep the kids company.

The Christian family is a mother and father with children, all living, laughing, loving, working, playing, struggling, and achieving together for the glory of God.

You must have a vision bigger than the here and now. You are not preparing your children for time, but for eternity. Adam begat a son in his own likeness. You will beget sons and daughters in your image. All earthly endeavors should anticipate eternity. As your child bears the image of his earthly parents, he must be caused to bear the image of his Heavenly Father. Born first in your image, he must be born again into Christ's image. For each child to be conformed to the image of God's Son is your expectation and hope. It is a colossal ambition, but you have the promises and resources of heaven at your disposal.

Wisdom is given upon request. Love is the highest commandment; self is our greatest enemy; the Bible is our only educational resource; the Holy Spirit is our comforter and teacher; the blood of Christ is our only hope of eternal life. Run the race that is set before you, *"forasmuch as ye know that your labour is not in vain in the Lord"* (1 Cor. 15:58).

LETTER FROM MOM TO THE GIRLS (BY DEBI PEARL, 1994)

Rebekah, Shalom, and Shoshanna,

Life is full of choices. There are choices you will make while you are still young that will help fashion your life as well as that of your children. Helping you prepare to make wise decisions has been our goal.

God said of Abraham, *"For I know him, that he will command his children and his household after him, and they shall keep the way of the LORD, to do justice and judgment; that the LORD may bring upon Abraham that which he hath spoken of him"* (Gen. 18:19). Preachers have often pondered why God chose Abraham to be the father of the Jewish nation. **God knew Abraham would** *"command his children"* (teach them to walk uprightly).

When the time comes for you to consider marriage, think about this: can this young man be trusted with God's heritage? It is not only your life he will touch, but the lives of your children and your children's children. Abraham's teaching was so effective that his son Isaac was willing to trust his father and submit to the sacrificial knife. Again, Isaac showed absolute confidence in his father's judgment when Abraham sent a servant to his kindred to choose a wife for him. Abraham knew it would take a chosen woman for the chosen man to continue the lineage God had begun.

Remember to be a helper to your husband. Stand behind your man with prayer, encouragement, and trust. Honor him, bless him, and serve him as unto the Lord. He will thrive before God in this environment. As he grows, your children will grow, and your cup will be so full that it will overflow into the lives of many others.

When you are peeved with him for some silly offense, remember, you are cutting off the prayer line. Don't allow hurt feelings to fester and disease the relationship. Be cheerful, thankful, and ready to forgive. Your children will watch you. If you show disregard, disapproval, anger, irritation, or dishonor to your husband, it will open the door for the children to do the same—not only to their father, but, in a greater degree, to you. In Proverbs it speaks of this very thing: *"Every wise woman buildeth her house: but the foolish plucketh it down with her hands"* (Prov. 14:1).

Begin training your children early; don't wait until there is a problem. A one-year-old baby who hesitates before obeying is developing a habit that will bring grief as he gets older. What your child is at two, he will be at twelve, only magnified many times over. *"Even a child is known by his doings, whether his work be pure, and whether it be right"* (Prov. 20:11). Don't expect your child to suddenly grow into a God-fearing adult. Adults spend their lives living out their formative years. *Adults are just old children.*

Don't let the cares of the family, the church, and the world steal the time needed to maintain holy matrimony. The time spent being a good wife is the deep root that nourishes the whole plant. Have a sanctuary where no child is allowed. There are times when being a good mother means teaching the children that, "This is OUR time, and you had better find something to occupy you elsewhere."

CONCLUDING THOUGHTS BY DEBI PEARL

All that you have been reading is what we have put into practice in rearing our children. But the reality is that you can rear happy, obedient, temperate, even God-fearing children who are still lost and undone before God. There is more to knowing God than techniques and principles and attitudes. There has to be that living, breathing life that only the Holy Spirit of God can give, and He has chosen you both as His channels to administer it to your children.

Do not get caught up in pouring your life into a good cause—even the rearing of a large family. Pour your life into knowing and serving the Savior and desiring that every life you touch be touched with the knowledge of forgiveness in the shed blood of Jesus.

We are called to be soldiers in the army of the living God. Raising up young new recruits is exciting. Children who see God in action, saving souls and changing lives, are seeing something real, something eternal.

When one of our daughters came back from a missionary trip to Central America, I asked her about the missionaries' children. Her reply startled me. She said: "The missionaries' kids have a vision to be the one to reach the next tribe. They are aware of the lost and dying tribe with no one to go to them unless they fill the gap. They spend their youth preparing and planning for that tribe. They know what they want to be when they grow up. They want to be the one who breaks the language barrier and tells that tribe the story of Christ in their own language. They grow up with purpose—the desire that those who have never heard might hear through them."

CHAPTER 25

Conclusion
by Michael Pearl

I have had many despondent-looking parents say to me, "I have waited too long. My children are too old to train." It is true that the older children get, the harder it is to mold them. Yet no human being ever gets too old to have his actions conditioned—as military boot camps demonstrate. But only in a controlled environment where the threat of force is real can a rebel be brought to bay. When a child gets old enough to seriously contemplate leaving home, the power of discipline will lose its effectiveness. You may not be able to recover everything with a fourteen-year-old, but you can see such improvement as to make it seem a miracle. The ten-year-old is still quite moldable. The earlier you start, the better, but as long as they live, it is never too late.

It is likely that one parent is going to read this book and revamp the training and discipline methods of the home, while the other may be content to continue with the status quo. Mother, if you decide to stop giving the children "chances," while your husband continues to play the threatening game, you will be tempted to have critical feelings. That will be your pride manifesting itself. Your bitterness at your husband and the obvious division that the children can detect will make matters worse. Your husband's pride will cause him to be even more resistant, lest he be the disciple of his critical wife and some unknown author.

Let me illustrate this by rating child training on a scale of one to ten— ten being the best. Now, if a mother who rated nine, while her husband only rated seven, were to make the children aware that she was not pleased with their father's level-seven child training, the children would suffer more than if both parents were at a non-critical level three—well below average.

There is nothing more damaging to the children than a divided, contentious authority. Blessed is the child who has two parents who love and enjoy each other without criticism, regardless of the level of their wisdom to train children.

Mother, if you know that you are the wiser one, a number nine, while your husband is a number three, there is a way to train your children and not allow the differences to be apparent to the children. Mind your own business in child training, and make your husband envious of your results. While your husband is away, be so consistent and thorough that you gain perfect, instant obedience from your children. Do not strive with your husband. Don't demand cooperation. Train them while he is gone. Spank them when he is away. They will learn that no matter how careless Daddy is, Mama is the "law of God Himself." Once you are in charge, when you see him failing to gain obedience, at an appropriate time, in his presence, quietly command the children, and they will run to obedience. After several days of this, he will ask, "How do you do it; they don't obey me that way?" Just humbly smile as you hold up the switch and say, *"The rod and reproof give wisdom"* (Prov. 29:15). Then demurely turn and walk away. He will become jealous—the good kind!

If you are not critical—and only if you are not critical—he will want to know more of your secret. The change in your attitude toward the children (no more anger, no arguments, quiet control) will get your husband's attention and actually please him! However, if the only change he sees is that you are spanking the children more, and in equal proportions you are angry with him, he will think it is just a hormonal imbalance that will hopefully run its course.

FINALLY . . .

Reading back over the text, I recognize that I have given a lot of negatives—what *not* to do, and what is *wrong*. If I were simply giving instructions for laying out a flower garden, it could all be done quite positively; but if a surgeon is instructing student doctors on heart surgery, there will be a lot of negatives. A procedure so invasive requires cautious, narrow limitations with needful—even dire—warnings. That which is successfully accomplished every day can end in tragedy if done negligently. Child rearing is an invasive procedure. You are invading the depths of a developing human being, an eternal living soul. It is not an inconsequential procedure. The whole heavens stand in the waiting room in anticipation of the safe delivery.

If after reading this you feel frustrated and discouraged, don't attempt to implement these techniques. This is not something that can be TRIED or applied a little at a time. It shouldn't be started and then stopped and re-tried again. It takes insight and confidence to endure. If this is all new to you and you have some doubts, you will not make it through the trials. You should read it again and follow it up with our books, *No Greater Joy Volume One, Volume Two,* and *Volume Three.* There is still plenty of time left in the lives of your children.

On the other hand, if I have put into words the things you have known all along but have never been able to articulate, and these concepts are in your heart, and you are totally convinced of the rightness of what we have said, then by God's grace you *will* see results.

Let me close with the words of a four-year-old. A family who had been applying these truths for only a week was visiting us in our front yard. Preparing to leave, the father called their new dog. The excited dog teased the man by running off just as he got within reach. The father became irritable and started speaking critically of the dog's intelligence. Pleading on behalf of the dog, his four-year-old son said, "But Daddy, you haven't trained him yet!"

And he shall turn the heart
of the fathers to the children,
and the heart of the children to their fathers,
lest I come and smite the earth
with a curse.

Malachi 4:6

Twenty-One Years Later (2015)

Michael and Debi

In 1994 when we first published *To Train Up a Child,* we had no idea that it would be so popular and would turn into a full-time ministry. We have now sold over 1.2 million copies. It is sold in Arabic, Chinese, Croatian, German, Korean, Tok Pisin (New Guinea trade language), Portuguese, Romanian, Russian, Spanish, Ukrainian, and more. Many additional books have been written and received wide acceptance. In 2014 we sold more books in China than we did in the U.S. We have been blessed with thousands of letters from parents around the world who have read this book and implemented its teachings. We join them in thanking God for his blessings upon their families.

Many children have written us, thanking us for the change in their parents. Wives testify that their marriages were restored when they got their children in order. Husbands have learned what they failed to learn from their own parents, and so have become better fathers.

When we first recommended this teaching to you, our children were not yet grown, and some of our readers doubted that the fruit would endure. But now that our children are all grown and have children of their own, we continue to reap the blessings of having trained up our children in the way they should go. God promises us in Proverbs 22:6, *"Train up a child in the way he should go: and when he is old, he will not depart from it."* None of our children have ever departed from walking in truth, and they are training their children as they were trained. Now that we have 22 grandchildren and more on the way, we have shifted from the role of parents to being "Mama Pearl" and "Big Papa." That means the kids get to go home at night.

Just as the Word of God predicted, our children have risen up and called us blessed (Prov. 31:28). To see them walking in truth, and to know that they are training their children as we trained them is the sweetest blessing of all. I am now teaching grandkids to swim and fish. Deb is already training the little girls to be good wives and mothers.

We have come to know hundreds of young people personally, many of them now married with children of their own, who were raised in a home where this book was a prominent part of their parents' library. They are now raising their children as they were raised, homeschooling them, spending lots of time with them, and being proactive in their training. The sweet fruit is flowing into the next generation.

The Family

These are the Pearl kids back when they were on the cutting edge of the homeschool movement. Left to right: Rebekah, 13; Shalom, 6; Nathan, 9; Shoshanna, 4 and Gabriel, 11.

Mama and Papa Pearl with some of their grandkids.

I have no greater joy than to hear
that my children walk in truth.

3 John 4

Product Catalog

Further reading and study materials by Michael and Debi Pearl

Training Children to Be Strong in Spirit

God clearly favors or likes some people over all others. Noah, Abraham, Ruth, David, Job, Samuel, and Daniel all found special favor with God. We are not talking about God having a warm and fuzzy feeling for them, but of treating them in a favorable way—an insider relationship, if you will. Abraham was "called the friend of God." John was "the disciple whom Jesus loved." And the other eleven disciples knew he enjoyed that special distinction.

Wouldn't it be great to be able to make simple changes in how you raise your children and thereby put them in the stream of God's special favor and blessing? And, in addition, think of training your children so that in the here and now, and throughout life, they attract the favor of others. You can do it.

This book tells you how. 200-page book.

Jumping Ship

There is a troubling trend showing up among some of the "homeschool crowd." Their children are discontent and rebellious, jumping ship as soon as they think they can survive without the family—some as young as sixteen years old. Michael Pearl addressed this issue in a series of NGJ magazine articles in 2006. These have now been compiled into this book, along with new material and an additional two chapters covering further issues. 106-page book. Available in English and Spanish.

Created to Be His Help Meet

What God is doing through this book is amazing. Has it provoked you to want to be the help meet God created you to be? We pray so. If it has blessed you (and your beloved) then consider passing the blessing on to someone you love by purchasing Created To Be His Help Meet for them. Available in: single volumes, cases of 24 (40% discount) and as an audio book on CD. 296-page book. Available in English or Spanish.

Preparing to Be A Help Meet

Being a good help meet starts long before marriage. It is a mindset, a learned habit, a way of life established as a young unmarried girl—or at least that's the way it should be. It is the older women who have experienced the joys of a good marriage whom God has appointed to pass along his instructions. That is what Debi Pearl has done in this new book. Preparing To Be A Help Meet also contains six sweet love stories written by wives sharing their experiences about how God taught them to be the help meets they are today. For unmarried and married women. 296-page book. Available in: single volumes, cases of 24 (40% discount) and as an audio book on CD. Available in English or Spanish.

– A reader writes:

"I love this book! As a wife it inspires me to be the woman my husband fell in love with. And I'm so excited to be able to share this wisdom with young girls. I can't wait to start a Bible study!"

Created to Need A Help Meet

All men know that they need their wives sexually. What most men don't know is that they need their wives emotionally, spiritually and mentally in order to be well-rounded, thoughtful, balanced and motivated men. You will be a better man once you come to see the whole truth concerning this matter. If you are a man, this book is for you. An Amazon reviewer called it a "...gritty, witty, no-holds-barred excursion into relationships and marital bliss." 248-page book. Available in: single volumes, cases of 24 (40% discount) and as an audio book on CD.

In Search of A Help Meet

Choosing your life's partner is one of the most important and lifedirecting decision you'll ever make. This book may save you from making the biggest mistake of your life. 248-page book. Available in: single volumes, cases of 24 (40% discount) and as an audio book on CD.

Samuel Learns To Yell & Tell

A child predator loses his power when he loses his cover. This story was written to teach children and parents this critical fact. It is written in a musical rhyme and rhythm that children love. They will also be more inclined to remember what they read by this type of writing. It is told in a simple story telling manner introducing a delightful young boy named Samuel to lead the way. 40-page full color book.

Sara Sue Learns To Yell & Tell

Debi's second book in Yell & Tell series! Join Sara Sue and her little sister as they continue to teach children to yell and tell. 40-page full color book.

Children as young as four years old through pre-teens will find these stories captivating, as well as instructional. If all children knew that they would be heard and protected when they yelled and told, it would stop most predators from child hunting. This book will equip parents and children to arm themselves against predators.

No Greater Joy Vol. 1

Reprints of the first two years of No Greater Joy articles. Covers the subjects of sibling rivalry, pouting, bad attitudes, and much more. 104-page book.

No Greater Joy Vol. 2

Let your children listen to great bedtime stories. Covers the subjects of rowdy boys, homeschooling, grief, and much more. 106-page book.

No Greater Joy Vol. 3

Children learn wisdom and enjoy listening to the stories as you read to them volumes 1, 2, and 3. Covers the subjects of marriage relationships and how they affect children, joy, much more. 103-page book.

The Joy of Training

Michael and Debi Pearl tell how they successfully trained up their five children with love, humor, the rod, and a King James Bible. The 2 DVD set contains the same high quality, digitally filmed content as the video set and hundreds of snapshots and video clips of family and children, illustrating the things being taught. 2 DVD set.

Teaching Responsibility

The difference between a man and a boy, no matter how old, is his willingness to bear his responsibility. In this seminar, Michael Pearl uses humorous stories and practical examples to illustrate the simple process of training your children to work without complaint. Cut into his speaking presentation are hundreds of video clips and photos that help illustrate his message. 2 DVD set.

Child Training 101

This message takes the viewer back to the basics. If you want to introduce child-training principles to a friend, this professionally-produced DVD will make a great impact. 1 DVD.

FREE Magazine Subscription

No Greater Joy Ministries Inc. publishes a bimonthly magazine with timely articles, stories, etc. Sign up online at **www.nogreaterjoy.org** or send your name and mailing address to No Greater Joy Ministries, 1000 Pearl Road, Pleasantville, TN 37033. Your information is confidential. We do not share your information with anyone.

If you are on our mailing list, you will also receive notification of when the Pearls are speaking in your area.

Free Online Resources!

Log on to **www.nogreaterjoy.org** for free Bible-study downloads, podcasts and articles on everything from child-training to homemade herbal tinctures. Sign up to recieve our email notifications to hear about specials, and you will also get a special word from Mike and Deb from time to time.

Go to **www.nogreaterjoy.org/magazine/free-subscription/online-notices/**

View and order our products at our online Store or call our toll-free order line at **866-292-9936**, 8 a.m. – 5 p.m. CST.

NGJ is a 501(c)3 Non-profit organization dedicated to serving families with the good news of Jesus Christ.